A BETTER CLASS OF BLOND

A Better Class of Blond

A California Diary

David Rees

Olive Press

First published in 1985 by The Olive Press,
Flat 2, 92 Great Titchfield Street, London, W1

© David Rees 1985

Text and cover design by David Williams
Cover photo from "A Bigger Splash" by Jack Hazan, © Jack Hazan
and Buzzy Enterprises, with kind permission by the film maker

Typeset by Wayside Graphics, Clevedon, Avon
Printed in Great Britain

ISBN 0 946889 04 X (pbk)
ISBN 0 946889 07 4 (hbk)

For Tom Holt, with love

The clouds are lifting from the high sierras,
The Bay mists clearing;
And the angel in the gate, the flowering plum,
Dances like Italy, imagining red.

—Louis Simpson, "Walt Whitman at Bear Mountain"

I

ICELAND. All mud it appears to be, though I know it is not. Mud scribbled on, incomprehensible hieroglyphics. Then Greenland: rock: a more solid chunk of Planet Earth. Icebergs! Scores of them. The *Titanic* is somewhere down there, under that turquoise glassy sea. Icefloes; from this height, soapflakes on water. Baffin Island. Flat, with pools that are perfectly round and ochre in colour, blobs of fresh paint dropped from the sky. We buck wildly over the Hudson Bay: a momentary turbulence, but I think of forced landings. On the blue un-wrinkled sheet below that would not be delightful; the cold would kill as quickly as this aircraft on fire. I glimpse almost nothing of the North American mainland, for the steward orders me to pull down the blind; the other passengers want to see the film. Do they? No one's opinion has been asked. Anyway, there's cloud beneath, nothing of interest. But I decide to be annoyed.

Two years ago the same destination, but another route, another me: another country, and, besides, the wench is dead . . . dry dazzle of the Great Salt Desert; snow-capped sierras—hands raised in supplication or benign gestures of blessing.

San Francisco ahead in a sunset that after all these hours and time zones seems eternal; the Pacific beyond, and beyond that surely the edge, the end of the world.

AT SF INTERNATIONAL a welcoming cavalcade. Dennis, Alan, Paul and Nils in a Cadillac Fleetwood Brougham d'Élégance, vast as a hearse and with more dials and gadgets than a 747 cockpit. Alan, still a twinkling Khruschev, is in leather and chains. "Madam, your chauf*feur*," he says, and bows.

"He thinks he's an English butler," Nils informs me.

Laughter and hugs and kisses, and how was the flight, and the weather this summer in the Peninsula has been just *awful*; the hetero crowd of families waiting for taxis and buses looks at us with mild disgust. Later, at Dennis and Paul's eating dinner, two years are swapped, chewed over, laughed at, and it seems impossible I should ever have been away, finding lovers and moving house, meeting people and writing books, living and partly living. I've simply come out for an evening with old friends and I'll drive home at midnight. But home is six thousand miles off, half the world away.

It takes a long time to become acclimatized. I've brought summer with me, apparently, and—it's never happened before—the heat bothers me. "The temperature in downtown San José is ninety-seven degrees . . ." I have a tummy bug. And my body clock, more obstinate than most, persists, a week later, in telling me it's past midnight when it's 4 p.m. So I sleep badly. And these dear good friends fill me with too much alcohol. I could say no, of course. There are always choices. Aren't there?

A crisis of confidence, too. Can I cope with a *whole year* in California? Teaching at an American university: what is expected of me? At home I know the corners to cut and not to cut. Not here. And will I find a lover? Or a year of bath-houses and tricks on Castro? Which do I want? For days I do nothing but sit on the deck at Dennis and Paul's, and we talk and eat and drink and listen. Mothy velvet evenings: drifts of flower scents, a paper lantern moon, Oakland lights flickering on the Bay's far shore. Talk and eat and drink and listen: we're experts. I can't rouse myself to find what's on offer in Castro; two years back I couldn't wait. When did I last have sex? A week ago, in London, with Ulrich. "You won't have your reputation absolutely wrecked by missing out on a few days," Paul observes. There's truth in that.

They've been together for twenty-six years. Retired from work now. Only in San Francisco have I met these stable relationships that span a quarter of a century: Sin City isn't all a brief suck. The one aspect of their lives I do not envy is they don't always know how to fill up the days.

On the deck sipping gin. Below, two cats frolic in the garden. Humming-birds flutter at the flowers. Swallows wheel and swoop, dart at insects, wheel and swoop again or squat on the power lines. They're practising; soon they'll be flying south. In this heat it doesn't seem probable, but already the globe is tilting towards fall.

I DRIVE round San Francisco, revisiting old haunts. Yes, it *is* one of the world's most beautiful cities, the most exciting place of all to work and play and live in. My memory hasn't fooled me. The coloured Victorians bright as a child's paint-box; the cable cars innocent adult toys. Fog pushes in from the ocean, huge waves of it rolling over the hills like Hawaiian surf, dissolving as the city's heat touches. The Bay's sheer sweep and size! So white boats at this distance are kids' paper yachts, busy for no seeming purpose. Moments when there is a real lift of the spirits: on Hyde by the Crookedest Street in the World, gazing down a hill so perpendicular you'd think the car would take off like a gull and land on Alcatraz. Or driving over the Golden Gate, again awed by size and sweep: its majestic simplicity. The view back from Marin: miles of dancing blue water to downtown San Francisco all cubes and turrets of glittering white—Leggoville. The Bay Bridge—can it *really* be so long? Why doesn't it sag or snap? I feel daft with enchantment, under a spell, in a sweet dream.

Fresh clear air. But on Castro I once or twice sniff the unpleasant odour of drains. The Village looks much as it ever did. Someone for everyone, the department store to suit all tastes, all on parade where 18th crosses; or they loll against the window-sills of Hibernia Beach, stand at bus stops where few people are really waiting for a bus. The traffic sign, the yellow diamond, has the same significance as our red triangle, a warning: halt, or falling rocks, etcetera. On Castro is America's only yellow diamond that says CLONES CROSSING. But the famous graffiti on Market has gone—a Moral Majority jerk sprayed in aerosol: IF GOD INTENDED GAYS HE WOULD HAVE CREATED ADAM AND BRUCE. Underneath it someone wrote in a different hue: HE DID.

The bars: the Pendulum, Badlands, the Village, the Elephant Walk, Twin Peaks, the Café San Marcos, Moby Dick, Castro Station, the Midnight Sun. Love for sale. And not for sale; but

[3]

to be enjoyed, free, for an hour, or perhaps—there's always a chance—for a life-time.

Tour operators now send coaches of old ladies of both sexes from Pasadena or Pittsburg to see Castro as they would the Statue of Liberty or the Grand Canyon. There's not much to see, of course—bars, restaurants, shops, dog turd on the sidewalks. But there are men looking and deciding, kissing and caressing on the street, in the open air, in full daylight. Not the same as a trip to Niagara.

There's more of it to observe than in any other ghetto, a gay this and a gay that which you don't find elsewhere—a florist, a card shop, a bakery where you can have your birthday cake iced with pink cocks or black jock-straps. San Francisco, I'm told, has seventeen gay traditional jazz bands. And one of the matches a gay softball team has every year is with the police. Yes, it's different from Earl's Court, and it's visible to the beady eye of the Pasadena lady.

I go into the Elephant Walk and order an orange juice.

WELL . . . THE TRICK is very, very me. I've not been in the Elephant Walk five minutes and I'm still absorbing the details of its remodelling when he comes up and says "Is that seat taken?"

Oh yes, just how I want a man: male male; long curly blond hair whitened by summer sun; skin very brown; blue eyes— startlingly, piercingly blue; fit, muscly, physical. Blond all over? He's from Santa Monica and missing the surf; no, he's never been to England but hopes one day to take a vacation in Europe; his job is working in a bar and he has, well, maybe two or three hours to spare.

To put it mildly, I'm not disappointed. The body is perfect. He *is* blond all over; the tan is all over. His cock is identical with mine in length, width and shape. My long-lost twin! And I'd thought no two were ever the same.

Gentle slow exploration of another's geography. He is much more interested in me than in his own immediate satisfaction, so I have all the time I want to please him. He's enjoying that. I don't know which way round it will be eventually, but it doesn't matter. He's lifting my legs over his shoulders, then he's inside

[4]

me, wild no-holds-barred screwing now, and he's arched his back so he can suck me off. Our noise will bring in the neighbours! Nestling into his arms, trying to touch with the maximum of skin. Silence, except for our breath. A dry wind outside.

I want to see him again; I want the phone number. But he's not too keen; a live-in lover who can be unpleasantly jealous. So he says.

SPEARFISH, SOUTH DAKOTA. Now this really is an odd story. Five years ago my ex-wife and I took part in a documentary for CBS Television about the problems of marriages in which one partner is homosexual. Three couples were involved. The first pair were so bitter they never met or spoke to each other; the second had stayed under the same roof but the man went off to trick on a Friday night and returned for Sunday brunch. We occupied the middle ground—divorced, in separate establishments, but keeping, by and large, on good terms. The film was not shown on British TV. Gary, a mixed-up unhappy boy of seventeen in Omaha, Nebraska, saw it and it changed his life: he wasn't, he realized, alone, unique. And he fell in love with that screen image of me. He obtained a copy of the programme from CBS, played it through endlessly. All he could learn was my name, that I lived in Exeter, England, and that I was a teacher. He contacted the Devon Education Office and asked for prospectuses of all the city's schools to try and find my address. So one morning years after the film, in my mail at the university, I found a letter from Spearfish, South Dakota. "You don't know me, but I know you . . ." Now twenty-one, he'd had affairs and slept around, but he always told the guys who came on too strong that his real lover was a British teacher he'd never met, and that if one day, by some utterly remote chance, he did meet this man, why, then there was no chance for anyone else.

A neurotic nut? I answered, of course. It was too intriguing to let pass. Why not, I suggested, send me a picture if you write again? A second letter duly arrived, at home this time. I remember going sleepily downstairs to pick up the mail and feeling the envelope: yes, it seemed to contain a photograph. This is where my interest abruptly ends, I thought; he's bound

[5]

to be hideous. Never have I been more wrong! Blond, blond, blond, a gorgeously better class of blond, male and hunky with a beautiful face and well-developed body. On a bed, naked.

The correspondence continued, needless to say. I thought him lonely, vulnerable, nice, and desperately wanting love. He's a student now, at college in Spearfish, SD, training to teach handicapped children.

My plans to spend a year in California were in no way influenced by all this, but I wrote to Gary to tell him that it was likely we'd meet at last. I gave him Dennis and Paul's phone number, and a picture of me. I got no reply.

"It's for you," Paul says, handing me the phone.

"David? Guess who I am."

He's working in a restaurant in Spearfish till term starts. We talk for a long while about nothing in particular, and produce no answer to the problem of how, or when, or where. Spearfish is a thousand miles east of San Francisco. But he likes the picture of me . . . yes, it's kinda . . . *definitely* OK! He hadn't answered because it arrived when he was on vacation in Colorado.

Dennis and Paul are fascinated, not only by the plot so far, but by what should happen next. About which they vigorously disagree. Dennis, optimist, romantic, says I don't start work for two weeks; why not fly up to Spearfish, or ask him down here? Paul looks Spearfish up in an atlas and tells us its population is three thousand and two, so it can't possess an airport for sure. And maybe this kid is an axe murderer. And the picture he sent is of his lover or his cousin, or torn out of a wank mag. Dennis says to call Republic Airlines and find out the cost of a ticket to Rapid City, which, Paul's atlas shows, is the nearest airport to Spearfish.

"Rapid City!" Paul scoffs. "What goddam names they have up there! Primitive, with no bathrooms, and Indians stabbing fish in water-holes. And South Dakota is only wonderful if you're *deeply* into wheatfields."

I disappear to telephone, and get several prices for San Francisco to Rapid City. You can't fly direct, but have to change at Minneapolis or Salt Lake or Las Vegas, and even the cheapest figure quoted is more than I can reasonably afford.

"Three hundred and twenty-five dollars!" Paul says. "The

most expensive cocks on Castro, the most delectable buns on Castro, are much less than that!"

Dennis tells him not to be so fucking cynical, and suggests I call the kid to ask will he split the fare with me.

"I'm in the middle of writing you a letter!" Gary says. If I come up, he explains, he can't spend too much time with me because of his work at the restaurant, and with me he wants *all* day, not just part of it. He'd rather come down to the Peninsula, for he's never been to Sin City—indeed any big city. But we *will* meet, he says. After so long, he can put up with a little more delay: he's learned he can't have everything *now*. At least we've heard each other's voices. "I've never spoken to a guy with an accent like yours," he says. "I've never met anyone British!"

Paul says it's far too exciting, so to avoid a complete nervous breakdown, he will have to fix cocktails, though it's only 10.30 in the morning. A bilious shade of bright green they are, strong, with lots of ice, and by noon we feel not paralytic but unfit for much else than drinking more of the stuff.

I look at Paul's atlas. Those South Dakota names aren't primitive, but romantic, impossibly far off. Deadwood. Hot Springs. Camp Crook. Like Chimborazo, Cotopaxi, Popocatépetl.

II

THE FIRST TIME I saw the Pacific Ocean I was, unlike stout Cortez, disappointed. It looked just like any other sea. Thinking, however, I should give it another chance, I drive down the Junipero Serra Freeway, and almost immediately outside the city limits the landscape becomes wild and beautiful. Earthquake country. On my right is the San Andreas Fault—a chain of lakes here, reservoirs containing most of San Francisco's water supply. Should doomsday happen, the flooding could be terrible. But you learn to live with earth tremors in California, and become as sanguine as we in England are about woodworm and rising damp. I woke once at 5 a.m. to hear all the beams in the apartment creak, the windows shiver, and I thought "Oh, it's an earthquake." And went back to sleep. Then there was the nice lady librarian who told me the Hayward Fault ran under the cellar of her house. One really bad shudder had cracked the chimney-breast from floor to ceiling. Didn't she know the danger, I asked, before she bought the place? Well, yes, she replied, but there were people living all along the street, and they seemed happy enough.

Above the San Andreas the hills rise, their slopes dark with fir and eucalyptus, and late in the afternoon the fog can shroud the peaks, thick and so dazzling white that you imagine you're gazing at Alpine snow. Today there is no fog: hot, a cloudless sky. On the left of the freeway is the huge ugly statue of Father Junipero Serra, one finger pointing, as if to warn, at the fault-line; and a rest station, an a.y.o.r. cruising area. I'm told it's now very risky—the police patrol it too often. I met a kid here once; he led me inside the statue (there is, appropriately—or was—a big hole at the base of its spine) and we kissed, took off each other's clothes, and fucked, under Father Junipero's concrete Franciscan skirts.

[8]

I drive across the San Andreas into the hills, then wind slowly down to the sea. I'm looking for the gay nude beach at San Gregorio, but I'm not sure of its precise location: it could be anywhere along this dramatic empty coast of shattered cliffs. Every strand and cove looks deserted, despite the glorious weather; in this bit of California people seem as sparse as in the west of Ireland. I walk some way along the cliffs, fearful of rattlesnakes in the dry scrubby vegetation, and eventually scramble down to the sea. Where I stay till sunset. There are only six people on this great stretch of beach: two men, nude, obviously lovers; and three girls and a boy in swimming costumes. Is this the famous gay San Gregorio? I don't know and I don't much care, lying naked in the sand, my skin caressed by a soft warm wind. The sea is rough, great frothy surf waves that remind me of Devon or Cornwall, and as the sun moves across the sky the sheen on the water is pewter. It's just like being at home, and I think of childhood years in the West Country or hot summer days only two weeks ago. Yes, one sea *is* much like another, and that's not disappointing: it's reassuring.

A NIGHT OUT IN SAN FRANCISCO. It's as lovely after dark as it is during the day; again, geography is the great asset. You're always aware of the city's edges. London has no frontiers, only horizons of houses. And if you drove out to those houses, you'd know that there are still houses up to the next sky-line. And beyond that. Here there is shape, pattern; water the frontier on three sides, hills on the fourth.

Chains of light mark out the streets, and the moving lights are traffic on the Bay Bridge: Sin City beckons. Castro and 18th are crowded of course, and so are the bars, but I'm not in the mood for alcohol or chatting a guy up, not in the frame of mind to go home at 3 a.m., drink-silly or perhaps rejected. I want sex *now*. So it's the wild back room of the Jaguar, where thirty or forty men are hunting. One Latino kid looks superb—slim, tall, with big black eyes, high cheek-bones and dark hair. His cock is being sucked by a man kneeling on the floor, and five others are just about to move in on the act. I join in too and he seems to like me; he's jerking me off—I'm upright as a telegraph pole. We kiss, and I run my fingers over his body. Young firm muscle

[9]

and skin; smooth, smooth. I bite his nipples and he moans with pleasure. The man on the floor is still sucking, and mouth after mouth is lubricating my cock. I nearly come, but pull away; it's too soon. I get behind the boy and he pushes his buns down over my cock; I wrap my legs round his and twisting his tits as hard as he'll take, I shove up inside and fuck like mad. Come, and stay, throbbing, till his shoots in whatever mouth, and he gasps; his body shudders, sweats. And he turns, subsides on my shoulder, his mouth looking for mine. A long, long, sweet kiss. "Thanks, kid," he whispers. "It was great!" And a guy, watching us, says "Beautiful. Beautiful!"

I'm home at midnight.

I want a lover, a kid like that, maybe. Who was he, where does he live, what is his job, is he amusing, intelligent? I must admit, however, I do find anonymous sex orgies in back rooms and bath-houses a turn-on, even if at times they leave me sad, as a one-night stand can do, the good experience as well as the unpleasant. I've had my share of unpleasant experiences; several, here in San Francisco, last visit. The drunk black who thieved my silver bracelet, the dishy blond who stole twenty dollars.

And there can't be a more likely situation than an orgy to get AIDS, herpes, NSU, syphilis, hepatitis, gonorrhoea, etcetera, etcetera, etcetera . . .

"DENNIS, THE SWALLOWS have gone," Paul says.

"Have they paid the rent?"

"No. Bunch of ass-holes!"

A year of teaching, sun worship, travel. And I have a full writing programme. Editorial changes in a novel, agreed but not yet done; short stories to think of let alone put into words; this diary; a commission to write a volume of essays on children's authors, accepted a year ago and not properly started. A lover would help. A young man sharing my room, the same young man tonight as yesterday and tomorrow, with whom I can swop the working day's idle gossip at dusk, curl round in bed, and when I wake in the small hours hear him breathe. And we'd screw, each and every revolution of the planet.

Paul shouts from the kitchen. "Dennis, do you think the little ones made it?"

"Well . . . they got to the Bayshore Freeway, I guess."

"Where they lift up their cute sexy wings and hitch a ride?"

Today I'm going south, like the swallows. Only fifty-five miles, to Los Gatos, where I can rent a room till next summer in a house owned by two women. But I'm saying farewell to these good friends who've fed and alcoholed me since I arrived. Sad and joky, as with the departed birds.

LOS GATOS. An old rambling timber house, room after room full of books and friendly worn furniture, a little untidy and much lived in. I'm in a far corner of it, a cool, shady place with a big double bed. A floor-to-ceiling window I can use as entry and exit. The garden is large, has a swimming pool, and so many trees that fences are invisible: we could be lost in woods. But are not, being on the extreme edge of town—one way, hills (fault-lines, rattlesnakes, tarantulas, black widow spiders); the other, San José and its satellites, a vast, sprawling mass that stretches for miles. I'm not so sure about the other inhabitants, however. A young couple, straight, unmarried, live in the garden cottage: they're fearsomely intellectual; she violist in the Santa Cruz Symphony and he majoring in Wittgenstein. Of the dykes, Sarah is big, soft, and sympathetic, but Harriet, who was married and has four grown-up children all living away with their live-ins, has lots of chips. She appears dissatisfied with everything and everyone. She doesn't consider herself as lesbian, though she and Sarah have been together for thirteen years. She sometimes goes off with men—and other women. An ardent feminist, and—I'm amused—she dislikes gay males. Why, I ask. Because they won't want *me*, she answers: though I don't dislike you; you have good vibes. Or is it that she instantly finds me unattractive? I don't sense that. Perhaps *attractive*? There's a challenge here. Sexual, emotional, intellectual—I'm not sure which—but it's a challenge I'll turn my back on. I don't want to know.

They're away for a week at Mammoth, and I'm house-sitting and dog-sitting. The dog and I soon come to an agreed *modus vivendi*: in exchange for walks, food, sleeping in my room at

[11]

night and pats on the head, it leaves me in peace for hours. So there is silence and slow time: by the pool's edge I write for much of the day, sweat, become bronzed in this ninety-degree heat, and plunge into the tepid water.

I walk the dog up into the hills, terrified of every ssssss I hear in the undergrowth. But these noises are lizards, and I gradually learn not to be alarmed. Our route, most days, takes us through the grounds of a Jesuit monastery. The priests' main activity, Harriet says, is their vineyard. For years they have been trying to turn a totally awful, undrinkable wine into one that is now drinkable but very poor indeed; as a consequence the monastery is full of red-faced jovial clerics smashed out of their tiny minds all day long. Drunk as a skunk monks. Perhaps she's right; I can't tell because I never see one. Early morning joggers, yes. Sloshed friars, no.

Interesting vegetation: blackberry, escallonia and marigold are obviously familiar, but there is poison oak, eucalyptus, and very southern-looking cypresses and pines. The most common weed is fennel: its sharp stink fills the air. The really striking difference between this and England, however, is the dryness of it all. No rain since March: the grass is withered and leaves are limp and dusty. There are fields here where horses live, but they're fed on hay.

The dog and I climb up to a school built by the Jesuits. It was shut years ago; there aren't enough children who want to make the trek up the hillside these days. Yet someone has turned on the sprinklers; lawns and oleander flourish. There is a magnificent view of San José on its flat plain with the parched, burnished Santa Clara Mountains beyond. You can't see much of the city, for downtown is covered in smog and the suburban houses are hidden by trees. It's like a mini Los Angeles. Only one buiding stands out; it looks like a Greek temple. For a moment I'm struck by the similarity not to LA, but to modern Athens.

It's clouding over. Intricate patterns, fish scales or white paint potato prints. But to no purpose—it won't be wet till November. Tonight the crickets will bleep-bleep as usual, like a zillion radio signals from outer galaxies.

GARY RINGS FROM SPEARFISH. He's lonely and sad: in Rapid

City a one-night stand is so rapid and so strictly for just one night. He ended with a lover two months back, a kid, a nineteen-year-old. I was bored, he says. The kid has no past, nothing of interest. His friends all laugh when he tells them he wants an older man, wants to settle down, find support and love, share a home, a life. You're young, they say; enjoy yourself. But is sex with as many different men as you can get enjoyment?

Of course it can be, but I don't tell him that.

I have a past. The dykes and I agreed that it was good to have a past, to be the sum total of what one was.

I have a month's holiday at Christmas, I say to Gary. I'll come up to Spearfish and sweep you off your feet. I'm easily swept, he says, laughing. And I'm an experienced broom, I add. I'm already swept, he replies. Into bed with me, I hope, is my answer. Oh, yes, he says, yes . . . please . . .

THE NINTH ANNUAL CASTRO STREET FAIR. Market, Castro and 18th are closed to traffic. There are stalls in the middle of the streets selling every conceivable kind of junk, from quilted pot-holders to stained glass and ceramic vases. Political booths—the gay Republicans (not much of a crowd at this one) and the gay Democrats, information desks, a mobile VD clinic, beer stalls, hot dog stalls, lost and found children. And entertainment: an official opening to the fair by that well-known drag nun, Sister Boom-Boom of the Sisters of Perpetual Indulgence, followed by cabaret from Sister Media and the Cassettes. Half an hour late this, a bit inefficient and not very original. The nuns seem to have got their loudspeaker wires twisted up with their wimples. I wander away, and find the professional standards of the San Francisco Gay Freedom Day Marching Band and Twirling Corps rather more impressive. But it's the crowd itself that is the real delight. Twenty thousand says the *Chronicle* next day; one hundred thousand claim the organizers.

It's a huge drag show: heavy leather, bare buns, construction gear, a centaur, a delicious blond in nothing but vine leaves, a hunk in nothing but chains, Roman togas, ballet dancers, bishops, cowboys. And drag queens; how many men are women and how many women are men? The star of it all is a guy who

[13]

spends hours leaning on a parking meter drinking can after can of beer, a beatific smile on his face. His head-dress is a stuffed pheasant with deer antlers from which quails' eggs dangle.

Not everyone is gay. There are plenty of straight couples, families, and tourists taking photographs. But it must, nevertheless, be one of the biggest gay gatherings in the world. Warm, friendly, amateur . . . and the cruising . . .

"Which side of the bed do you like to sleep?" asks this terribly polite Chinese kid.

"That side."

"Would you prefer tea or coffee in the morning?"

"I don't mind. Coffee."

"With milk?"

"Please."

"And sugar?"

"No thanks." I laugh. "Has the inquisition ended?"

"One more question." He grins. "What do you want to do to me in bed?"

"Fuck you."

Which is entirely satisfactory for the two bodies concerned. And their minds: next day we both feel good, very relaxed. Kid! He's thirty-three, a well-to-do dress designer from Quebec, and his apartment is in Pacific Heights, upper-crust snob San Francisco. He has a lover, out of town for the weekend . . .

"But you have now experienced the joys of rice," Dennis says when I tell him.

IT'S THE JUNIPERO SERRA once more, and I'm driving back to Los Gatos. THE WORLD'S MOST BEAUTIFUL FREEWAY, a hoarding announces. Well . . . the M5 near Bristol is pretty spectacular, but, nevertheless, I'm enjoying the scenery very much and thinking about nothing special when, near Los Altos Hills, the car radio plays "When Will I See You Again?" And suddenly in my mind's eye is Andy, ex-lover and one of my closest friends. He lives in my house in England; occasionally he comes into my bed when Ulrich is absent and we make love, gentle and affectionate, as old friends should: I see him now at the moment of our parting, the night before I left for California, in London, in a street near Harpoon Louie's.

[14]

"I'll miss you more than you can ever know," he said.
I miss you too, Andy. A lot.

III

THE PHONE RINGS at 8 a.m. Dennis. "David, how did you like the earthquake?"

"What earthquake?"

"Last night, of course. The epicentre was at Freedom, near Watsonville, not far south of you. Jesus, you must be a heavy sleeper! It woke us up, and we're ninety miles away!"

"Was it severe? Anyone dead?"

"Four point five on the Richter scale, a medium sort of quake. No, no one died."

"The dog barked, about two o'clock. Was it then?"

"Yes. Your first earthquake this trip, and you sleep through it!"

The shock waves were felt along the San Andreas, which is half a mile from here. Cups smashed in downtown Los Gatos and beds slid across floors, but I felt nothing. It's the third jolt in the Bay Area this week, and I haven't sensed the slightest tremor. I'm disappointed.

I was surprised when I first visited San Francisco to see so much Victorian architecture; was all this rebuilt after 1906? No, I was told, it was never destroyed. The 1906 disaster affected only a small part of the city; the damage and loss of life was almost entirely the result of explosions in severed gas mains and fires caused by wrecked electricity cables. That couldn't happen now, people say—San Francisco has learned its lessons. Maybe the predictions of the horrors to come are the fulminations of those who see the place as a contemporary Sodom, who'd like it wiped off the map, evidence of the hand of the Lord punishing the unnatural. Castro, however, looks to me as if it's here to stay.

THE WEATHER turns out to be less reliable than those Victorian houses. Thunderclouds drift up from the Baja; a freak storm erupts at breakfast-time and lasts till noon. A really dramatic performance, this: crashing thunder overhead, lightning, heavy drenching rain. I'm walking the dog in the woods when it starts. What did I say earlier, that it wouldn't rain till November? Suddenly everything smells clean and sweet; the leaves have lost that grey dustiness, and I'm soaked to the skin.

AMERICAN BARS—often rooms without any character at all, their only redeeming feature the speed and efficiency of the people who work there. They can be ugly, depressing places: I long for the carpets of an English pub, the quiet corners with tables and chairs designed for conversation. I'd like my beer served in a glass instead of having to swig from the bottle, however macho that looks. Tricks in all the gay haunts if one wants them: but being gobbled in the back yard is limited fun. Why all this cock-sucking? I enjoy it as an exciting preliminary, not an end in itself; as I come in a mouth I think of what Oscar Wilde said about smoking—exquisite, but unsatisfying.

I did go to the wrong beach. Friends take me to the correct place, which is much like the other: unstable cliffs, a long sweep of sand, a turbulent sea. There's a huge quantity of driftwood, and over the years the patrons have dragged these bleached, torn branches above the highest tide mark and built them into shelters, little one-room cabins without roofs. Not so much to protect themselves from the wind, but in order to fashion a semi-private piece of terrain for making love. *Semi-private*: you can see everything that is going on if you care to look. The driftwood walls give the inhabitants the illusion of ownership, so you wouldn't attempt to join in unless you were invited. It would be like breaking into another man's bedroom.

It's foggy and cool today, but that seems to deter only the faint-hearted. To the inveterate cruiser, bad weather is of little consequence, even if he's shivering from head to foot, his cock shrivelled, his balls frozen. This beach is full of naked solitary danglers. They spend hours walking, staring, exchanging glances, never giving up hope, occasionally finding a willing

[17]

someone. Would they suffer the same discomfort in pursuit of anything else? I doubt it. The strength of the sex drive can make men ridiculous.

There isn't a great deal of action. A few lovers inside their wooden pallisades. They tolerate—maybe enjoy—the witnesses, but they don't invite more participants. If I were one of them, I wouldn't object to being watched, might even ask a third to our feast.

What I don't like is being a solitary dangler.

A COLLEAGUE AT THE UNIVERSITY writes me a note written on the back of a "Grade Review".

> I, the undersigned student, do not believe the grade given me on this essay is justified. Therefore I am requesting a review of my essay by my peers. I agree to accept their decision as final. For instance, if my instructor gave me a "C" and the class determines that I deserve a "B", then I will receive the "B". Likewise, however, if my instructor gave me a "C" and the class determines that I deserve a "D", then I will receive the "D". The grading criteria used will be those delineated on the sheet handed out by Mrs Horovitz at the beginning of the semester. The class responsible for the review will be Mrs Horovitz's other class, not the one I am enrolled in.

This is followed by spaces for the date, the student's and the instructor's signatures, the signature of two witnesses, the essay title, the grade given by the instructor, and the grade given by the class.

A British university would regard democracy of this sort as chaotic, a recipe for revolution. How is Mrs Horovitz to cope with her students if the grade is upped?

QUIET DAYS IN LOS GATOS. Warm enough to stand by the pool, sipping gin at ten in the evening, dressed only in shorts. My skin is golden brown. The girls have returned. We meet in the kitchen, the centre of this L-shaped house, or in the garden at the pool's edge. They let me lead my own existence. They swim at midnight, get drunk once in a while, walk for hours in

[18]

the hills, and—it's odd—work most evenings in separate rooms.

AT A DINNER PARTY I meet another David, good-looking, male male; a respiratory specialist at a hospital. Twenty-seven. His marriage has just broken up; he's slowly and carefully coming to terms with being homosexual. Sounds like *Making Love* (a movie I thoroughly enjoyed; the husband and wife scenes when he told her the truth were painfully authentic.)

"You're an extremely attractive man," I say, and he's kissing me. If he's going to do anything, he says more than once, it will be with me.

Hmmm.

Gary writes from Spearfish: "I wish I knew what the future holds. David? My friends think I act like I'm in love with you. And I don't even know the guy. All I say is yes I do."

Hmmm.

ANTS MARCH IN COLUMNS HERE, chomp-chomp-chomp-chomp, as in cartoon films. I think of Andy's dislike of them, how I'd tease him they'd advance on the kitchen, military fashion, and destroy our precious home-grown veg and fruit . . .

At last I meet one of the monks. He's in mufti and smoking the most enormous cigar I've ever seen. A Corona Corona, the sort that requires both hands to hold it. We talk of Reagan and Thatcher, the idiocy of the Falklands war. I'm disappointed he's not as blotto as Harriet says they always are; stone cold sober in fact.

"What's that thing you're wearing round your neck?" he asks. He's hoping it will be a Christopher, a cross, some Catholic talisman.

"Taurus the Bull," I inform him . . .

Sarah looks up from the paper at breakfast and says "Another earthquake yesterday, the fourth this week."

"What's it all mean?" I ask.

"There's two different theories, both diametrically opposed. One group of experts thinks it's a good sign: a lot of little quakes ease the pressure. The other party believes they're the preliminary to the big bang."

We discuss for a while how nice it would be if an earthquake blew up the university; we'd not have to teach for months. And would this house stand in a repeat of 1906: it wouldn't, she decides . . .

Why am I so down? Recording this trivia, opting for living so quietly? The two women are oppressive. And I'm not well; I'm exhausted, mentally and physically. It might be roses if I had a lover in my bed.

Sanity begins in the cock. Doesn't it?

MORE STRANGE MEMOS at the university. This is from the president, no less. The president—vice-chancellor in our terms—is a woman: has any British university ever appointed one?

> On August 11 1982 the California State University requirement to fingerprint all new employees was abolished and in the future the decision to fingerprint or not to fingerprint is delegated to each campus president. It is my decision to eliminate the fingerprinting requirement at San José . . .

PETER ARRIVES FROM ENGLAND for the Gay Olympic Games. He's never been to the West Coast before and he's as bubbly with excitement as I was two years ago. I catch up on the latest Brit. gay lit. gossip; drive him round the switchbacks of San Francisco and he's enchanted with cable cars and glimpses of Alcatraz. He assumes I'm having a wonderful time: I tell him I'm not, that I'm listless, without energy, exhausted.

We're lucky: a fantastic sunset from Marin, Leggo City over the water glittering gold, sky colours dissolving through every shade of orange, purple, pink. Then a tour of Castro dives. Contrasts: the Café San Marcos does have carpets and tables and a certain elegance; we can sit quietly and talk. Badlands— Sadlands—is dimly lit, dingy, loud, full of bodies. I've never seen people cruising in Sadlands, busy though it often can be. The patrons are mostly alone, and they just stand there, jigging to the music, wrapped in their own private fantasies. They never look at anyone else.

"It reminds me," Peter says, "of comments and attitudes

in—say—the 1940s: the twilight world." These tags—"the homosexual subculture", "the demi-monde"—that suggest gays are inevitably doomed to self-hatred and unhappiness seem, in this bar, to have a certain truth. Some of us cannot help rushing into straitjackets straights invent, just as the Jews, admiring German efficiency, quietly entered the gas chambers.

The Midnight Sun. You're bound to get picked up in here if you want to; and soon I'm talking with, and being kissed by, this blond—Wendell. Bright, amusing, intelligent. A lawyer. He's meeting his room-mate, but let's do something tomorrow afternoon, he says; he'll give me a call at 10.30. He writes down my number. He doesn't want us to go home to his place now: last week he answered the door and two men with sawn-off shotguns burst in and robbed him. He's scared to sleep there at night; every little noise and he's sweating with fear. He's looking for another apartment, needless to say.

Peter and I return to the San Marcos where we talk to three Swedes now settled in California. Eventually Peter goes home, and I'm in a quandary. The Swedes want me to go to the End-up disco; Peter wants me to meet him at ten o'clock tomorrow morning so I can get a Press pass for the opening ceremonies of the Olympics—he's covering it for *Gay News*; and the blond has said he'll ring at 10.30. The last is what I really want, so I drive to Los Gatos, randy and dissatisfied; and wake at seven with a rigid cock. Looking forward to the afternoon's pleasures, I ignore it. A mistake, of course. I knew it would be. As I write this it's half-past eleven and the phone has kept silent.

At which point it rings. It's him!

TAPIOLA ON THE CAR RADIO. I've loved Sibelius always, this piece as much as any. Not real forests, not real snowstorms, as Vivaldi's seasons are literal pictures in music, but the landscapes of the mind. I want my books, the California of this book, to be the landscape of *my* mind.

TELEPHONE CALLS, and Tim says to bring Wendell to Oakland for the party; Paul says to stop at his place—with Wendell—overnight. (Dennis is in Portland, Oregon.) Saturday, but my

[21]

blond is working till six; I'm to meet him at his office. No time for the opening of the Gay Games; I chat to Paul instead.

Six o'clock, and work not yet finished; he'll have to go in Sunday morning. He's edgy, hyper-active, and generally cross with life. But even better-looking than last night; I'm itching to get his clothes off.

"I can't face a party," he says. "Do you mind if I back out?" Yes, but I say it's OK. Come to his apartment at eleven, he suggests, but will I call him first when I'm leaving Tim's. He doesn't explain the significance of phoning, and I forget to do so.

Valencia and 14th: dubious territory. "I don't like it here," Paul wails. He locks both car doors and keeps the engine running while I walk down to the apartment. Rough, certainly; mean-looking blacks on the pavements. It's half an hour before midnight. I'm not scared. I ring the street-door bell; no answer. Then a woman opens it, a dog behind her; she's just going out, presumbly taking it for a walk.

"What do you want?" she asks. I explain. "Go on up," she says. "I don't know if he's in, but you can check it out."

I ring the apartment bell. A long silence. "Who is it?" someone shouts from inside.

"David."

Chains rattle, bolts slide, and there is Wendell and his roommate. I have never in my life seen two men so frightened. They'd thought it was the armed muggers making a second visit.

"Why didn't you call?" Wendell asks, again and again. "Then we'd have known it was you at the door! I thought you'd call an hour back, and when you didn't I assumed you weren't coming!"

They're almost incoherent and can't stand still for a moment: the adrenalin is racing so much. They tell me more about the robbery, and I begin to see why they're so terrified. The thieves—blacks—were looking for drugs and money, but got annoyed when they didn't find much of either. Mike and Wendell, forced to lie face down on the floor, were knocked about with the guns; the blacks then ripped the room apart. One of them said, prior to leaving, "Kill them both." He meant it, Mike emphasized; all witnesses would then be removed. But an unexpected noise—the cat jumping through the bedroom window—alarmed them, and they fled.

"Why are you so sure they'll return?" I ask.

"Because we're here!" Wendell says. "Alive! They'll want to rub out the evidence—*us*!"

He feels guilty about leaving Mike, but Mike insists he's OK; he's taken a sleeping pill, he's drowsy already, he'll bolt, lock, chain, and barricade the door after we've left.

It takes an hour and several glasses of Paul's whisky for Wendell to calm down, but at last we're in bed. I'm sleepy and I've been drinking; I'm afraid I'll be limp. But no problem. Hairy blond all over, suntanned—and he fucks superbly. God, I *needed* that! Orgasms the same split second. We smoke, drink bourbon, and talk till half past three.

He's really life in the fast lane: listening to him is an education in the worst aspects of America I've read about so often and never bumped into. He's been mugged three times before, twice in New York and once in San Francisco. He was knocked about so violently that he has a permanent neck injury, a lot of pain. In New York, one of the muggers was a man he picked up for sex: afterwards this guy—a black—tied him to the bed, explained how to undo the knots (it would take ten minutes at least) and left him sixty cents to get the bus to work. "I have to admit," Wendell says, with a rueful grin, "that he screwed fantastically!" He's been on all the drugs at one time or another, including acid. Still on coke. San Francisco, he reckons, is nastier than New York. Life here is cheap, dangerous, and brutal. Behind the experienced face (he's thirty, I guess) and the tired, cornflower-colour eyes I can glimpse the innocent country boy from Wyoming he must have been ten years ago.

He lived with Gerald—another black—for four years. "I loved him. Totally. I gave him everything. He screwed around and gave me all the venereal diseases you can think of. Now he's got Kaposi's sarcoma." Wendell, two years after the break-up, is still very bitter. "I hate him! *Hate* him!"

I sleep as I sleep with Ulrich, wrapped round him like a question mark. He jabbers in his dreams, once turning over to twist my left nipple and shout "Are you satisfied? Eh? Are you

[23]

satisfied?" By seven the sun is so brilliant I can't even doze. I suck his cock and he smiles, opens his eyes; his face is lit up with pleasure. This time I screw him. Orgasm, once more, at exactly the same moment. As far as sex is concerned, we're a perfect match.

I drive him to his office, then go back to Paul's. Cute, lively, interesting, is Paul's verdict. No mean commendation; he's a born cynic.

"Do you want to see him again?" he asks.

"I guess."

"And . . . ?"

"I suggested next weekend. He'd like to go out into the country, he said, so I offered Los Gatos, the swimming pool, but he didn't jump at the idea."

"You made love *twice?* And talked for ages, afterwards, both times? Of course he wants to see you again! I bet you he calls."

He doesn't. I call him. Nothing.

More than "When will I see you again?" is will I see England again? I've observed no violence, but I read of it in the papers, hear of it constantly on the radio, and my friends talk of it much more than they used to. Wendell's experience isn't unique— many guys I know in California have been mugged or burgled. The editor of the *Castro Times* was held up at knife-point and robbed last week in broad daylight. The street was busy; people eating in the deli looked out of the window and watched, but none of them came to his assistance. And Castro is not a violent area. Muggings and rapes on the university campus at San José: when I go to my night class on Tuesdays, Sarah advises, park the car at the nearest point to my room and don't dawdle. San Francisco has had thirty-four murders committed by handguns in the last twelve months; Great Britain eight. Yet not many Californians agree with Mayor Feinstein's new law forbidding the carrying of handguns. Some of this fear is neurotic. A parallel: everyone I talk to knows a man who has died or is dying of Kaposi's sarcoma, but there are only eighty-eight recorded deaths from this disease in the whole of America. Fear is infectious, and though I wasn't scared on 14th last night, I'm bothered by what I'm told and what I read. The instability of the earth's crust worries me less than the instability of people.

Wendell's life-style isn't in any way mine. I'd soon get disenchanted with the pace, the freneticism. And I can't deal with a coke addict.

IV

THE NEWSPAPERS PUBLISH an opinion poll on creationism: ninety-one per cent of those interviewed believe that God created man, or that he evolved, guided by God. Only nine per cent, therefore, are atheist or agnostic. No wonder this country seems weird.

I TALK FOR A COUPLE OF HOURS with Julian, who is a colleague at the university, a writer, gay, and Tim's ex-lover. He thinks gay publishing in Britain is at the moment healthy and more exciting than it is in the States. At least a British editor reads your manuscripts and gives you his opinion, he says. Here they don't.

If your lover, he informs me, is years younger than you, the attraction on his part derives from a lack of structure in himself: he's drawn towards someone who is, apparently, structured. You can spend three, five, eight years giving him the structure he needs, then he leaves you. And when you're away from home, don't imagine everyone and everything back there is standing still. You return to changes you hadn't foreseen and don't like. He's commenting on his own current set-up, but . . . well . . . it gives me pause for thought.

PERFECT SEPTEMBER WEATHER. Cloudless days, eighty-five degrees of heat and not a trace of humidity. The beaches are without fog and I make for San Gregorio, only thirty miles from here, but I have to cross mountain passes as high as Snowdon. My gas guzzler doesn't like it, and nor do I: the vertical drops on the bends into nothing but fresh air are terrifying. I have to concentrate so hard that I don't take in much of the scenery, but my mind snapshots towering redwoods in great caverns of forest gloom, the withered yellow grass of summits where sunlight hurts, glimpses of the distant Pacific so pale blue I feel thirsty.

The beach is busy today. I sit in my driftwood cabin and exchange smiles with the passers-by. And eventually I'm talking to a man who's not blond, not young, but probably my age; he's been married too, and has a daughter aged nine. We share our pasts over home-made cookies and fruit juice. Some months ago the one gay relationship he's had broke up. In the early evening, when the crowd has thinned, we make love. Sand, salt. He has some baby oil in his pack. The sun is a dazzling gold causeway on the sea.

I drive home, a longer but much less tortuous route, feeling at peace with the world. A spectacular view of the Bay at nightfall, the Santa Clara Mountains burnt, smudgy and tired from the heat. Papery, like a child's painting. Lights of the Bay cities more than a thousand feet below me: Saratoga, Cupertino, Palo Alto, San Mateo. Chimborazo, Cotopaxi . . .

ODD, DRIVING TO BUY MILK in the nearest supermarket in Los Gatos, that I cross from one of the earth's geographical plates to another. There ought to be some profound sense of change—or at least a marker, a sign-post. Nothing. The Santa Cruz Freeway roars under the bridge, along the fault-line.

WITH PETER TO THE CLOSING ceremonies of the Gay Olympics. A crowd of about twelve thousand in San Francisco's Kezar Stadium, a tremendous atmosphere of excitement and celebration. An event about which I'll be glad to say, afterwards, I was there—even though the athletes parade round the track to, of all things, *Pomp and Circumstance Number One*. I see from the programme that Mayor Feinstein has officially proclaimed this week "Gay Games Week" and asks all the citizens of San Francisco to take note of the fact. Could this happen anywhere else in the world? She isn't here, though. But our Congressman is. He needs the gay vote, of course, but in his speech he goes further than he has to, saying he's pledged to fight all forms of anti-gay discrimination, particularly—it's the matter of the moment—the court order banning our use of the word "Olympics". And he outlines precisely what he intends to do—quite unlike a British politician.

[27]

A lot of speakers. Rita Mae Brown says blonds are like gays: they usually have a better time of it. Hmmm. The homophobe is a "spiritual fascist", but the famous who cower in the closet receive the brunt of her anger: "You find them in sport too, in tennis . . ." Uproar. Cheers, laughter, chants of "Martina! Martina!" When she can resume, she says "They are liars, particularly to themselves; they are bent on self-destruction, and they particularly hate people like us." I agree, as I do with Tom Waddell, the organizer of this first Olympiad, who says "We must fight with love because love is what we're best at."

The finale is a gigantic disco on the grass, athletes as well as spectators joining in. Much more pleasant than a dimly lit club. Why do we have to put up with so much bordello illumination in our bars and discos? I guess it's to pull in those who feel they're unattractive, those who are comfortable only when partially seen. I'm struck on this occasion by how beautiful the men and women are, dancing in their tee-shirts and shorts (there's no drag of any kind today), and how good it is to see them in their thousands, just enjoying themselves. I dance with a blond hairdresser from Berkeley (whose lover pulls him angrily away), with a blond athlete from Los Angeles (he's wearing his silver medal), then with Dan, the blond barman I met in the Elephant Walk. He's delighted to see me. How have I been? How's the teaching? How's Los Gatos? He's moving back to Santa Monica—the surf tugs more powerfully than the delights of this city. He really *is* beautiful. Long, long, curly hair, and fantastic blue eyes. He's dressed only in shorts and a garland of flowers— the last of the hippies.

As I drive to his apartment on this day of heat and sunshine, and look from the hills at the coloured city beneath, I find it impossible to imagine violence and brutality can exist here.

Sex leaves me still on a high: to be fucked by a man as beautiful and as good at it as this one is just leaves me feeling . . . privileged. Next week he'll have gone south; and I don't suppose I shall ever see him again. But that doesn't destroy my mood.

Harriet brings me down to earth. What's the point of it all, she asks. Gay Games, what do you hope to achieve? Aren't there any gay people in the *real* Olympics? I try to tell her, but it's useless. And she spends nearly every night in bed with someone of her own sex!

LOS GATOS IS SPANISH for *the cats*. Why, I ask, give a place such a strange name? Because, Harriet says, to service the prospectors in the Gold Rush days, the biggest cat-house in the West was built here. It's as likely a story as her drunk monks. The oldest house in town, Sarah tells me, has two big stone cats at its gates—hence Los Gatos.

The heat disturbs my nights. A hundred degrees at noon yesterday—OK. But bad dreams wake me in the small hours. Or is it mosquitoes, or because the other half of the bed is empty? I listen to the far-off barking of dogs, and return to sleep only by wrapping my arms and legs round pillows, thinking blond.

Gary calls and invites me to Spearfish for Thanksgiving. Ten weeks away. I am definitely one of his long-term options, he says. The others aren't men—they're places and jobs. I could be someone by a road-sign at which he pauses, he tells me, but perhaps we'll travel together. Women in the last century answered advertisements for marriage in Australia, sailed out there and lived happily ever after.

Three in the morning. Crickets. There's a strong wind to-night, but it brings no lessening of the heat. The wood of the house groans, snaps like gunshots. An earth tremor?

THE BATHS. The Watergarden, San José, to be precise, dearer than most similar establishments, but very de luxe. Some very de luxe men, too. I've been often recently because there are always attractive bodies who want to be screwed rigid—into the floor, as they say. Some quite splendidly expert Vietnamese kids. We have more choice than straights when it comes to what we do in bed—one of the bonuses of being gay is the variety of roles we can assume. It's possible, of course, for a woman to make love with a man aggressively, for the man to be led the whole time, but we can move further, from the most macho games to complete passivity—and all the different fulfilments in between. The straight guy knows none of the delights of being penetrated. Manhandled. I've enjoyed being screwed quite savagely at times, and the bigger the cock the bigger the chal-

[29]

lenge, the excitement—though gargantua does not necessarily provide the ultimate in bliss. I had a relationship that lasted seven years, and in bed he wanted to do little else than fuck. Whatever satisfaction—emotional and physical—it gave me, I was not doing what I wanted most of all, which is to screw. That imbalance contributed to the downfall of things. For me, the most pleasure and what leaves me feeling a hundred per cent sane, whole, and good to be alive, is when he is on his back and my cock is inside him, particularly if he is slim, bond, youthful and masculine, lets me be quite rough with my teeth on his neck, wants my hand to twist his nipples till they hurt, while my other hand, KY slippery, manipulates his cock. And if the cock isn't too small. And orgasm is more or less simultaneous . . . a lot of ifs!

He has to be male male: an effeminate man gives me instant limpness. It's not the buns that turn me on, though that's where my cock wants to go, and they can be aesthetically beautiful. It's the maleness of shoulder-blades, biceps that curve impressively, chest and thigh muscles that are the result of strenuous physical exercise: that's when I start getting hard. I can't imagine, now, the pleasure of penetrating a woman. All that softness. And no cock. It would be a totally alien landscape.

TO LOS DESPERADOS, the local gay disco. I sense at once that this isn't cruising ground, let alone where I'll find undying love; the problem is everybody knows everybody else. Your friendly neighbourhood gay bar . . . the one that has no time for strangers. They're all with their own crowd. If this was Salt Lake City, I'd be in the middle of three conversations at once; the bars there don't see a tourist in a hundred years. Well, that has been my experience. But Los Gatos is not in Utah, not quite so remote and certainly not Mormonized; it's on the edge of a conurbation of nearly a million people, and San Francisco is an easy drive up the Peninsula. Los Desperados (far from desperate) is much like some of the clubs and discos in English provincial towns—good music, nice kids, pleasant decor—and cliquey. I leave after an hour or so, not having spoken to a soul.

COMMOTION AT 4 a.m.—we're torn from sleep by the sounds

[30]

of bodies plunging into the swimming pool. The dog is barking her head off. It may not mean that violent urban America has at last come to destroy Los Gatos, but it's undoubtedly an intruder. A very dark night; none of us feels we want to rush outside and make a citizen's arrest.

"Goddam teenage kids," Harriet says, and phones the police. Who arrive with incredible speed—in about three minutes. A car must have been patrolling down a road nearby. The two cops advance stealthily on the pool, waving guns and flashlights and shouting "Come on out of there at once!"

Our felons are a family of racoons.

Laughter, apologies, coffee all round, and back to bed.

NOT BECAUSE I SUSPECT I've caught something, but after all my recent escapades I think a check-up is a good idea. The only venereal disease I've ever had is NSU—I've been lucky. Notoriously difficult to diagnose and cure, NSU: the symptoms are so mild. Is this slight burning another attack—or my imagination? Is that a discharge—or sperm from last night's sex?

I go to the Santa Clara Health Clinic, where I pay the required six dollars and fill up a long form that wants information about symptoms, what kind of sex I've had recently—gay or straight, oral or rectal, and so on—and partners (not much I can disclose: at the baths one rarely exchanges addresses and phone numbers, and I wouldn't know how to spell those Vietnamese names). Unlike England, it's mixed: there are no separate times for men and for women. But the crowd looks much like the crowd you'd find in any VD queue back home—that sounds ridiculous, but I'm sure there are various types of people you *don't* see in a special clinic; therefore some types you do: in my experience, amazingly dishy young men.

I'm interviewed at great length by a nice elderly woman clerk, who takes a blood sample and informs me that the clinic only treats, in its six-dollar fee, cases of gonorrhoea and syphilis: other venereal conditions are casualties of Reaganomics. I feel outraged. It's as if the government has said to the germs "Go forth and multiply." They presumably do.

I get passed on to the doctor, and perform the customary rituals—peeing in bottles, etcetera. There is no instant treatment here: the lab takes two days to analyse the specimens. They'll phone me on Wednesday if there's anything wrong. If I have NSU they'll tell me, but I'll have to pay extra for the antibiotics.

I have nothing.

JULIAN IS CHARGED with drunk driving. No bag of crystals in America: it's a blood test and he's sure he's not guilty—just two glasses of beer a couple of hours before the incident. The police saw him drive away without lights from a restaurant; he'd gone only one block when he remembered to switch them on, but it was already too late.

Why record this? I don't like the police anywhere. If they suspect you of an offence of any sort, they are extremely unpleasant, the British as much as all the others. But—in the Land of the Free—was it necessary to point guns at this mild, middle-aged university professor, handcuff him, verbally abuse him, hold him in jail overnight, take away his medicines (he's had a heart attack), and not let him know the result of the blood test so he can't tell how he should plead when the case comes up?

V

MONDAY MORNING, at work feeling as if I'm suffering from a bad hangover. Which is odd as I haven't been drinking. Tuesday afternoon, and my temperature is a hundred and two. Thursday evening I'm in hospital, having a lumbar puncture for suspected meningitis.

It isn't bacterial meningitis, but there's more than twice as much protein in my body as there should be. Jesus, am I *ill*! Unless I lie absolutely prone, I have a crippling headache. I vomit all over the neurologist's office. Then I'm sent to an isolation ward, where I'm drip-fed intravenously, a process that almost drives me to tears of frustration and anger—I cannot go to the loo without lugging this cumbersome machine with me, and it wakes me frequently at night, urging me to pee. I feel I'm a lavatory, being constantly flushed.

Light hurts. My temperature is a hundred and two for a whole week. Food is disgusting. Being pushed in a wheelchair makes me dizzy and sick, as if I'm in an aeroplane, spinning out of control. I'm not allowed to have any visitors. I'm given a brain scan, a chest X-ray, an EEG; innumerable blood samples are taken and analysed. The white corpuscle count is extremely low, and I've virtually stopped manufacturing platelets. A haematologist is called in. He diagnoses leukopenia (destruction of the leukocytes) and thrombocytopenia (inability of the blood to clot properly). There is also an excessive production of lymphocytes, some of them "bizarre", and a poor sedimentation rate. I don't know what all this means—except that my immune system is taking a battering from something very nasty.

The neurologist rules out brain tumours, lung cancer, diabetes and half a dozen other horrors, but he isn't really sure what is wrong with me. He thinks it is a flu virus that is, he says, "behaving unusually." He prescribes no medicines, not even to get the temperature down. But it does drop at last; I gradually recover and I'm sent home. I don't remember much of the ordeal, in particular *how* time has passed while I have been lying there. They've given me tylenol as a leaving present, for the headaches, which persist for several days. The newspapers are full of the tylenol–cyanide murders. (Someone, last month, put a number of tylenol—codeine—tablets, laced with cyanide, in Johnson and Johnson bottles and left them on the shelves of drug stores in Chicago. Seven people have died.)

The fever has gone, but I'm far from well. It's a weird condition, difficult to describe; the haematologist calls it fugue, but the neurologist says it can't be, as fugue means a severe memory loss. My senses seem to be dislocated. Taste and smell have returned to normal; I can bear kitchen and bathroom odours; and I have a positively gluttonous desire for bacon and eggs. How delicious my breakfasts have become! I don't usually enjoy a morning fry-up, though Ulrich and I sometimes had one at weekends; now, every day, bacon and eggs—and my pleasure in this is almost orgasmic. Harriet and Sarah invite me one evening to eat roast lamb with them, and I have four, five, greedy helpings; I could go on stuffing myself with it all night.

Balance, hearing, touch, eyesight are wrong. Everything I know to be flat slopes. Hearing—not so bad, but a symphony orchestra on the radio is a harsh, confused jangling. Touch—I have no urge whatsoever for sex. I masturbate once, just to make sure I still can, but there's no pleasure in it. Worst affected are the eyes. It's as if there is a veil or some kind of ectoplasm between me and everything, or Sylvia Plath's invisible bell-jar were incarcerating me. Some times are really bad—the landscape can dissolve in yellow dots, as it does when one faints. But I know I'm not going to faint.

Obviously I can't drive the car. I'm off work, more or less indefinitely: "Have another two weeks' rest," says the neurologist. "Do what you feel you can do." Days pass. Weeks. Moments of panic—I'll *never* be well again. I read, and write, for my book on children's authors, though I seem to have lost a sense of judgement, too. What are these essays on Jane Langton and Katherine Paterson worth? I don't know.

Ulrich sends flowers. "Get better soon. Missing you very much."

The weather saves me from almost crushing depression. Seventy, seventy-five degrees, cloudless, golden fall light; it's October, but feels as if we were living in perpetual September. I walk each morning and afternoon in the mountains and find, as with the bacon and eggs, that I need this weather, this landscape, almost sensually—the light, the leaves, the parched grasses, the skies, the huge vistas down to the Bay.

It's a month since I came out of hospital, and I'm still unfit. Bills from the doctors arrive with every post—thank God I'm insured; the brain scan alone cost four hundred and fifty dollars. I don't detect a great many differences between our socialist and their capitalist medicine, except cost. The treatment, the care and attention, the food, are about the same. Maybe, initially, you'll get seen more quickly here; I don't know, as I've never been an emergency case in England. I'm not sure how necessary all those tests were. In England, I imagine, the minimum would be done; here, as the patient pays rather than the state, the doctors perhaps do things our doctors would not. There's a lot of snobbery attached to American medicine— a great deal of money goes on plush offices ("suites" they're called) with sofas and potted plants all over the place, on immaculate headed writing paper, on clerical staff sending out bills.

I've got used to not working. To solitude. Bacon and eggs, this weather, are enough. As for that better class of blond: Gary writes and phones. So do Ulrich and Andy, but separation from them doesn't bother me. I'm more concerned with getting myself well—being unfugued. I'm zonked, exhausted, drained.

A MEETING OF GAY STUDENTS at the university. I feel distinctly uncomfortable because I'm not sure, being faculty, if I ought to be here, and nobody has said "Hi!" or "Who are you?" or "Come on in." In fact I'm ignored totally: very un-American—Americans are usually much more welcoming and friendly than we are. *I* of course could talk to *them*—but I'm so shaky I'm incapable of getting up from the cushions on which I've seated myself. Just driving the car ten miles has, for the moment, sapped all my energy.

But I must be improving. On the way home I want sex and spend some time at the Watergarden with a very satisfactory young body, firm and fit. One more slim Vietnamese boy.

So two gay events within a few hours of each other, and at neither have I spoken a word. I am not just an ageing face; I am not just a certain size of cock that likes to fuck rather roughly. I am these things, but more than these things. Gays can be guilty of synecdoche—or is it metonymy? I'm never sure of the difference. I'm referring to those figures of speech in which the part stands for the whole; "Give us this day our daily bread": bread means all our food, not just bread. If our search for the part—the big cock, the unlined face—becomes paramount, we can end up using only bits of ourselves, never being able to relate to the complexities of real people. And we then ossify. Become a living fragment of bone.

That "very satisfactory young body, firm and fit" and the "ageing face" also needed to talk, to go out to dinner, listen to a symphony concert . . . whatever. Anything rather than silence. I'm lonely tonight, and wish I were back in England, among friends.

A YOUNG MAN, A CAR MECHANIC, is stopped by the police because his tail-light is not working.

"Shit! And I've only just mended it," he says.

The cop obligingly holds a torch while the guy fiddles with the wires, then suddenly the cop starts viciously beating him over the head with the torch, yelling "Where's the gun? Come on, where's the gun?"

The car mechanic, head streaming with blood, says "There is no gun!"

And indeed there is not. The policeman apologises and drives off.

TROUBLE BETWEEN HARRIET AND SARAH, stemming, as I think it usually does, from Harriet's bisexuality. In Greece this summer she met a man, Konstantin, who is now staying at the house—Sarah is not thrilled. "There are ways of coping with jealousy," she says. "You don't own someone else's body."

But when she and Harriet think they're alone, you can hear them from the street, screaming and bawling at each other.

I don't blame Sarah one bit. Katya, who lives just round the corner and is a friend of both women, asks me what's going on. My opinion is the same as hers—open relationships are fine if the people concerned want that; but if one does and the other does not, then the person who screws around ought to be rather more discreet than Harriet is being. Katya and I admit, laughing—because it isn't totally logical—that we're envious of Harriet. Why should she have two lovers when we have none? We know, of course, only too well the longueurs of steady affairs; how much in Harriet's situation we might want excitement on the side, and—in contrast—how awful it can be if one's partner is doing it.

Katya, after two marriages and seven children, has been alone for eighteen months. She's forty-nine, Russian, very sympathetic. "If he presented himself at my door with all the right credentials," she says, "I'd let him in. But I can't be bothered to go out and look. Not now." She sips her vodka, and gazes at the distant mountains. "Actually I don't think I want another man," she continues. "I'd prefer a woman." More gentleness possibly; more stability. Is that why? She's never had a lesbian relationship. "I miss sex," she says. "But not so much as curling up with someone in bed."

Eventually Konstantin departs. Maybe things will settle down, but Sarah and Harriet are not speaking to each other.

TWO LONG ARTICLES in the *San Francisco Chronicle* on AIDS, and a poll on whether the current scares about sexually transmitted diseases are causing gay men to change their life-styles. The fact that a hitherto unknown virus may be causing the collapse of the body's ability to deal with certain rare secondary infections—chiefly fungal conditions, Kaposi's sarcoma, pneumocystis carinii, and toxoplasmosis—which almost inevitably lead to death, is only now beginning to worry people. But what makes the immune system lose its ability to fight? Prime suspects are the herpes viruses. Hepatitis B is another possibility. Also the life-styles of the victims—men who frequently take poppers, cocaine and amphetamines, and who are sexually very promiscuous. The articles do not mention, however, that all known deaths from AIDS-related diseases, with three exceptions, have occurred in the United States. Some gay men in other countries also sniff poppers, sleep around, and are hepatitis sufferers. So far they have mysteriously escaped.

The poll's conclusions are that many of us are changing our life-styles. There is less promiscuity; we're returning to dating, staying with one partner, and not tricking. I hadn't noticed. The Watergarden, for example, is busy all week, every week.

I wonder if my illness wasn't some form of acquired immune deficiency. The signs—says the *Chronicle*—can be any combination of fevers that persist for four or five days, unexplained weight loss, flu symptoms, swollen lymph glands, herpes sores that don't heal, nerve damage, and bluish or purple spots on the skin. The first four in the list apply to me. I had recently been to the baths; the white corpuscle count dropped dramatically; and I'm not yet well. I've returned to work, still with eyesight and hearing problems. My classes occasionally disappear in a whirl of yellow dots, but I'm coping. Physical strength is returning slowly. The neurologist tells me the virus has damaged the middle ear; whether permanently or not is uncertain.

Was it AIDS?*

---

*It wasn't. If I had known then (October 1982) what I know now, I wouldn't have wondered for even a passing moment. It was not realized at the time—at least not by the general public—that the incubation period for AIDS is, at its most rapid, four months, and that usually it is one or two years before the victim has any of the symptoms. The AIDS fever resembles a mild attack of flu; there was definitely nothing mild about my illness.

The *Chronicle* reports were misleading: AIDS was not a subject that was unduly bothering the majority of gay men in San Francisco in the autumn of 1982. The bath-houses were still busy, and the Castro life-style in full swing. It was in the early months of 1983, when a sharp rise in the number of new cases—and deaths—occurred, that people began to be seriously alarmed. Between the spring and summer of 1983 media coverage was intense, and the general public, gay and straight, began to learn more about the symptoms of AIDS and what kind of sexual behaviour might lead to its spread.

The summer of 1983 saw something like a real AIDS panic in

America, resulting in a decline in the incidence of the better-known sexually transmitted diseases, as gays in their thousands either abandoned or cut down on promiscuity and stopped frequenting the bath-houses. When I left California in September that year, the expected further rise in the number of new cases of AIDS had not happened; and there was speculation that the virus could have mutated into a more benign form.

The suggestion that AIDS is somehow linked to drugs has now been largely discounted. It also seems unlikely that it has any direct connection with the herpes or hepatitis viruses, though it may well be that it finds an easy victim in a body that is already weakened by these illnesses and/or drug abuse.

My own sickness, I suspect, was something more serious than flu "behaving unusually", and though bacterial meningitis was ruled out, I feel the haematologist was probably correct when he told me that he thought it was *viral* meningitis.

VI

WAKING FROM A NIGHT of good sex to the unfamiliar surroundings of another man's room: what sort of a person is he? I glance at the books—Maurois, Gertrude Stein, *The Architectural Heritage of San Francisco*, *Everyday Life in Ancient China*. A bicycle, a TV, four jardinières with exotic plants suspended from the ceiling. He's still asleep. Good-looking. How many times have I found myself in a similar situation over the years? I couldn't begin to count.

At breakfast, desultory conversation. The ritual exchange of addresses and telephone numbers. He invites me to a Hallowe'en party. I think I'll go; I like him.

He's Vietnamese. Half-French, half-Vietnamese, to be exact—so taller than some Orientals and hairier on the legs, though his chest is smooth and the skin perfect. His name is Phil—Phillippe. Beautiful hazel eyes, high cheek-bones and sensual lips. A surprisingly big cock—thick, uncircumcised.

One of the boat people. An orphan at sixteen; his father, a schoolmaster, died in the war and his mother disappeared without trace. He lived for the next few years selling his body on the streets of Saigon. When the Communists arrived he fled, suffering unimaginable hardships on the boats. He nearly died of thirst. He works as a builder's labourer, which has given him a mature, muscular man's physique. Educated: well read, into ballet and classical music. But no qualifications—he can't get a more intellectual job despite fluent French and English. He's twenty-seven and lives in the spare room at Robert and Matt's—old friends of mine. I picked him up in the Elephant Walk.

My illness caused a six weeks' absence from San Francisco. On the deck at Robert and Matt's in the late October sunshine drinking coffee, talking, looking at their brilliant vivid flowers,

[40]

the coloured toy city spread out below us; we're all in shorts or just our underwear—it's still that hot. Eighty-two degrees. The best kind of lazy Sunday morning.

THE NEWS TONIGHT says that at least two people a day are being admitted to hospital with acquired immune deficiency illnesses; that it has begun to attack the straight population; and that two hundred and forty-nine deaths from all AIDS-related diseases have now occurred in the United States, thirty-five of them in San Francisco.

Perhaps because heterosexuals are now suffering, the authorities will pump money into research: it isn't just a matter, they may start to think, of a few promiscuous drug-mad faggots finding the fate they so richly deserve.

I'M MORE OR LESS back to normal. Occasional eyesight problems, nothing else.

PHIL. Fucking him was superb.

THE HOUSE IS SO QUIET. Sarah and Harriet only talk to each other when they have to; the quarrel rumbles on. "I must reorganize my life," Sarah says to me. "But how?" Harriet looks grim, and when she isn't at the university she lives almost entirely in her bedroom. "It could be worse," Sarah says, but her face suggests that it couldn't. Maybe my being around is a useful buffer; I don't know, for neither has poured out her troubles to me. Nor, as far as I can tell, to anyone else.

I'm getting fed up with it. Harriet only speaks to me in monosyllables. Sarah occasionally stops and chats, but I force her into those moments. They have remarkably little consideration for me, the third member of the household. I'd hoped to enjoy living with gay women. And learn something—I know few lesbians, none of them well. This opportunity . . . it's ceasing to be an opportunity.

Did Harriet fancy me? Sarah hinted that she did. Harriet's realized at last that I won't get into her bed? A selfish, immature person. She's treating me as if I were some kind of insect. She likes the rent money, of course.

I'd move out if I knew where to go.

DINNER WITH JULIAN. I enjoy these sessions; I've rarely met anyone with whom I have so much in common. Our conversation is mostly of relationships: the errors we made with lovers, why love ended, why nothing in the future will last. When I say that the pattern will not necessarily repeat itself, he's gently mocking. We *always* repeat ourselves, he says.

On the way home I listen to the old-fashioned, well-modulated tones of Quentin Crisp on the car radio. His voice is British movie actor of 1930s vintage. Hostesses like to invite a few gay friends to their parties, he says. We're so well behaved. So amusing. Because we're an unpopular minority, we have to work extra hard to be accepted. That's why we don't cause problems and why we enjoy entertaining others.

Yuck! What century, what sort of closet, does he think we live in?

A WEEKEND IN SAN FRANCISCO with Phil, who's quiet, gentle, amusing; it's good being in the city with another man who's not exactly an acquaintance, not yet a friend but a . . . lover? What word should I use? Friday we go to dinner with friends of his who live on Sanchez; Saturday we idle away a damp grey morning, eating a slow breakfast with Matt and Robert; the afternoon is spent drinking gin at Dennis and Paul's; and in the evening we eat out, Italian, at the Sausage Factory on Castro. It's Hallowe'en—the party he'd invited me to was postponed, so we wander up and down Castro and 18th, hand in hand, looking at people. By ten o'clock a big crowd has assembled, most of them in fantastic costume. It's even more of a carnival than the Street Fair, though nothing is organized by anyone: it's a spontaneous celebration. The crowd soon grows to a vast size and the cops appear, not to disperse us, but to close the street to traffic. Once again the Village makes its own rules and wins. "A perpetual circus," Dennis called it this afternoon. (He and Paul, just back from a trip to Puerto Rico, New York and Atlanta, were in great form despite bad colds and Paul having lost a front tooth eating muffins.)

I see witches on roller skates and a dozen Satans; a troupe of black men with spears and grass skirts war-dancing outside the Pendulum; a drag Marilyn Monroe whose gestures, arms and facial expressions are almost superior to the original; hundreds of ghouls, ghosts, spooks and spectres gibbering, squeaking and howling; even parrots, monkeys, a unicorn. In the Elephant Walk we meet up with Tim, Maureen, Matt, Robert, Nils and Alan (who's rather the worse for drink, in a sweet silly state; wearing a poncho and ostrich feathers so large he nearly removes several people's eyes). Parties in all the flats above the shops and bars, the guests thronging the windows and staring down at the street crowd which must now number thousands. Someone at a party pushes two loudspeakers on to the second-floor window-sills above Castro Station, and music is blasted into the crowd who all begin to dance: "I've really got it together; people will see me and cry . . . FAME!"

Sunday. The weather's cleared up; it's as hot as August. Phil and I go to a restaurant on 24th for brunch; November, and we're eating out of doors. Eggs benedict, and glasses of plum brandy mixed with cinzano. The whole city seems to want to eat out, fearing, perhaps, that it may be the last weekend before winter; so brunch queues everywhere, particularly for tables on side-walks and in gardens. What are they doing in London, I ask myself.

Later, we amble along the streets—shirtless, it's so warm—looking at shops and houses. Noe and 24th are all health foods, Eastern exotica, books on yoga and meditation; a whole store, gentle harp music on tape as you enter, is devoted to astral planes, star signs, supernatural knick-knackery. The houses: I have never seen a city that has so much beautiful, well-preserved, nineteenth-century domestic architecture as San Francisco. No house is of the same pattern or shape as any other; each is an individual creation. Street after street in Castro and Noe Valley is a delight to the eye. Trees, flowers, shrubs finish the picture. I could live here: with the right man, that better class of blond; a house on Noe or Castro or Douglass or 21st, 20th, 26th, Diamond, Valley, Elizabeth, Liberty, Sanchez, a score of others . . .

On the cliffs to the west of the Golden Gate this hot, sunny afternoon, high up above Land's End. The ground is tortured and fissured by mud-slides and earthquakes. A rough blue ocean crashes in white spray against the boulders. In the calm, on the other side of the Golden Gate, the little white yachts tack and drift. Where we are, seals bark. Sandpipers scurry after the waves with ludicrous speed on spindly legs. We lie on the rocks in each other's arms, exchanging biographies. He likes my body, he says many times; my muscles—the arms, legs, chest— "have good definition", he tells me. Nothing wrong with *his* definition. Sex this weekend has been . . . I can't think of a suitable superlative, and I realize, with some amusement, that I only record in this diary sex when it's good. Why haven't I mentioned the bad times? Want to forget them I suppose.

"I need," Phil says, "not the baths and the Castro life, but quote marriage unquote." What does he dream of with me? I'm a transient.

GARY PHONES at 6 a.m. His father has had a severe heart attack; he's returning to Omaha to be with Dad. I shan't be able to come to Spearfish for Thanksgiving.

NOVEMBER 2, 1982: mid-term elections. California shifts a little to the right—a Republican Governor and Senator are elected with tiny majorities. The nuclear freeze proposition is passed, but there's a resounding no to the idea of banning handguns. Presumably Californians hate dying in a nuclear holocaust, but they don't object to being shot dead in the streets.

At Katya's I watch it all on TV: the same excitement as at a British general election. The TV does it well, which surprises me, for news coverage on American television is abysmal compared with ours.

CARTER *v.* REAGAN: it was Tweedledum versus Tweedledummer.

I'VE MOVED OUT. Just down the road to Katya's, where I have a makeshift bed in the hall and very little room to store my property; but it's good to be in a friendly house with a congenial person who has time in the evenings for conversation and alcohol. I've said little about Katya, but I've spent many hours with her: except at weekends I'm at the university in the mornings; the afternoons are for writing; then when I've eaten I need to talk to another human being. Not possible with Harriet and Sarah—sulky, silent creatures shut in their separate rooms night after night. Katya is always ready to pause, as I am, in the evenings. She's radical, feminist, left wing, immensely curious about people, ideas, and literature. Together we've consumed gallons of wine—outside in her garden on hot summer nights, and recently in front of a roaring log fire.

Harriet gave me a month's notice. When I asked why, she said I'm too much in the house. My presence—even alone in my room, writing—upset her. I told her I was thinking of going anyway. Our standards of behaviour were very different, she said. She was referring to the fact that I smoke, and keep much later hours than she does. She can't complain of anything else. I've made little noise—no TV or record player in my room, and only twice have I entertained visitors. (With her permission, asked beforehand.) And not once have I had a man in for sex. Yes, I said, our standards of behaviour were indeed very different, and I did not need to stop for one second to consider which of the two codes of conduct was more moral. She and Sarah can now tear each other to pieces with only the young couple in the garden cottage—the violist and the Wittgenstein expert—to watch. They call the house "Saturday night at the fights."

Sarah, trying her utmost to keep the relationship going, did nothing to prevent my dismissal. If I were you, I said to her, I wouldn't feel comfortable about my role in all this. She was not, she told me. I understand her: years of her life have been put into Harriet-and-Sarah. Years, money, emotion. Though there is absolutely nothing left of love as far as I can see, and they would both be better off apart, to leave smacks of failure; at forty-two she finds the prospect of the unknown terrifying. To start again . . . she cannot do it, she thinks. But, like all the rest of us, she can if she has to.

Harriet is neurotic, unhappy, and reclusive. Alone some eighteen hours a day. Was she jealous of my friendship with Katya? Or my professional status? (Her appointment at the university is temporary—she can be fired at any time.) It was sex. She was wanting that when she let me have the room. When it dawned on her that I'd never, in a thousand years, screw her, she could only cope by turning nasty. Well . . . that's what I think.

She dislikes almost anyone of either sex who is not turned on by her attentions, so Katya—and others—tell me. The pleasures of friendship are therefore always denied her.

Is this a common problem for bisexuals?

VII

THE FIRST WEEK OF NOVEMBER was so warm I could work at the pool-side wearing only shorts. The second week is the coldest in the Peninsula since records began in the Gold Rush years. Last night the Los Gatos temperature fell to freezing-point; unheard of, everyone says. There is thick snow on the Santa Clara summits, and also behind us, on the Santa Cruz Mountains. Route 80, the main road that connects San Francisco with the rest of the world, is closed at the Donner Pass. I never thought to see snow in California in November! In the Bay area I never thought I'd see it at all.

But by Friday we have summer sunshine again, which lasts for my weekend in the city with Phil. A party at Tim's, a disco (the I-Beam), meals out in pleasant little restaurants. I feel very relaxed with Phil, enjoy his company, like his friends. And I like *him*. I can't find any faults—yet. Though vagueness, un-punctuality, slowness might irritate eventually. If we lived together I'd have to do all the cooking, which I would *not* enjoy. Why do people think I'm a good cook? I'm not. But Katya is enchanted with my meals! Her shopping-list relies heavily on bread, onions, and potatoes—and she boils up tea in a kettle, just as my Irish grandmother did. No wonder anyone else seems a good cook.

Moments with Phil when I experience an old, familiar sensa-tion—a curious slithering in the stomach, a surge of happiness. Falling in love? He's a very lovable person, which isn't quite the same thing. Gorgeous, dancing with him, though any good disco sweeps me off my feet. (A silly image. I was firmly *on* my feet. On top form, in fact, dancing bare to the waist, sweat pouring in buckets.) The I-Beam I haven't visited for two years: it hasn't changed a bit. Same lighting system, same old brown paint, probably the same music. Probably the same crowd of men.

I'd like to live in San Francisco next semester. With Phil? We don't know each other well enough to make decisions of that sort; I mustn't allow myself to be persuaded just because I'd like to live once again with a man: a recipe for disaster.

THE PROOFS OF MY NEW NOVEL, *The Estuary*, have arrived. The best bit of the writing process is reading the proofs; for the first time I can see my labours as a book: it's now a finished thing, no longer part of myself, gestating in the womb as it were; it's a new creature, almost born. It's still sufficiently in my head for what I had to say to seem important. But the bound, final version—the book itself—gives no excitement. It's too long since I wrote it; my mind has moved on to other things.

But one day I shall write a much better book. I have the experience; I have the language. I lack patience, the ability to reject ruthlessly, to rewrite and rewrite. It comes too easily and it's too enjoyable. I finish a novel in six months that ought to take six years. I don't let it *grow*. So what I want to say sticks out too baldly, doesn't filter up from the depths. There aren't enough layers.

I'M NEGLECTING THIS JOURNAL—no time now I'm living at Katya's, the weekends spent with Phil, reading for the book of essays I'm trying to write. And grading student papers. The boredom of that! Today we have grading of papers. Phil was here last night to dinner, to meet Katya. To prove good meals come from England I cook roast beef, but it isn't impressive. The Yorkshire pudding stubbornly refuses to rise.

A tremendous storm in the night. Heavy drenching rain, and a gale so strong the roots of the house move. I'm awake at five, listening. Or was it indigestion that disturbed me? I'm drinking too much white wine these days, and my stomach rebels. Phil sleeps through the storm, but uneasily; he turns, groping for my hand. Am I in his dream? At six Katya gets up, bangs windows shut, and goes to the kitchen to wash, noisily, last night's plates. She went to bed very early: leaving the lovers alone? It wasn't necessary. I think she didn't like Phil. Or . . . is she, too, sexually attracted? And therefore jealous? Maybe because it's happened once, I now see it where it is not. But when I told

Sarah I was moving in here, she said, with a funny little smirk, "That had better work out!" I didn't understand, and Katya, when I told her, said "Is that right? Whatever did she mean?" I don't want, a second time and so soon, to fall victim to another's jealousy: to take on the role of Joseph Andrews. Where are the uncomplicated friendships gay men have with women? Not to worry: when I've gone they'll settle back once more into the friendships they had with each other, Katya each day from March to November in Harriet's swimming pool.

And I will soon be gone. Phil and I have decided to look for an apartment in San Francisco, despite the inconvenience for me of the miles from work. In the big city we're happy; can be ourselves if we're not too far from Castro. I could write about the pleasures of last weekend, but I'd only be repeating myself: screwing, meals out, a film. A Britten concert: something very civilized about being in a warm church listening to the delicious clashing sounds of the *Missa Brevis* and the *Lachrymae*. Outside the sun shone, as it did all weekend, giving Sin City that appearance of looking, despite the chill winter wind, not far short of paradise.

The better class of blond, I have to report in the fall of 1982, is Vietnamese: an olive-skinned man with jet black hair who loves being fucked and who has a cock so attractive I can't keep my hands and mouth off it.

It is all moving too quickly.

AIMEZ-VOUS BRAHMS? The chamber music, yes; but not the symphonies. Musical to the finger-tips, structures as solid as buildings, the ability to pull a tune out of hints and fragments, a tune you didn't realize, previously, was there. But the *sempre dolce cantabile* and the thick muddy orchestration pall. He can never write anything *fast*. I've just been listening to the second symphony; the finale sounds like woolly mammoths trying to copulate: their sheer bulk stops them coming.

PHIL AND I GENTLY DRUNK on piña colada at Dennis and Paul's. Brunch at Maggie's on 24th. Making love. A game of bridge with six other men and Katya.

"Slow is best; slower is better," she says of me and Phil.

[49]

"*Festina lente*. Is he pompous? Lacking a sense of humour?" No. Definitely not. Castro shops now full of Christmas gaudiness: nude men on wrapping paper, soap stamped GAY BAR or shaped like cocks; mugs, tea-cloths, shirts with slogans, innuendoes, invitations. *Lohengrin* at San Francisco Opera: production, costumes, orchestral playing, singing excellent. Driving down the Junipero Serra on Monday morning, late for work.

That was my weekend.

A CARAFE OF WINE WITH JULIAN. A worrier, and always the fall guy, now fretting himself silly from reading about AIDS. He asks me for every minute detail of my illness; says I should check with the AIDS specialists in San Francisco that my immune system has not been radically altered. He wants to go to the baths, but daren't. More likely to get the clap, I tell him, but he's not reassured: gonorrhoea you can deal with; AIDS is another matter entirely. True. We swap details of memorable bath-house sex; both of us, for different reasons, wistful, as if we'll not do it again.

We talk about Katya. She's lonely, he emphasizes; I've become a surrogate husband. No surprise she doesn't like Phil— he means the end of my stay at her house. It's not sexual her interest in me—the company is what she values. And the help with gadgets—her left hand was permanently damaged in an accident.

He's right. Once more.

NOT A WORD FROM SPEARFISH for nearly a month, and I don't know the Omaha address. Perhaps he's found a lover. Is his father dead? On the road back to health? I still want to meet Gary. At least have one night with him.

THANKSGIVING. At Phil's, but not spending the day together; we both have prior arrangements that are too complex to change. So, on a morning of heat and sunshine like summer (it's difficult to imagine this is the last Thurday in November) I'm returning to Los Gatos for dinner with Katya, her seven children and their lovers/husbands/wives. Tonight they will all be in a row of sleeping-bags across the lounge floor. I'm not fond of turkey, but this is one of the best I've tasted, and the cranberry sauce—home-made, the fruit fresh-picked—is superb. A battery of vegetables. I try not to eat too much, for I have another Thanksgiving dinner this evening with my students.

A second turkey! A second battery of vegetables! I look at this meal without enthusiasm—but I manage. I skip the pumpkin pie and toy with a rich chocolate dessert. I've been drinking since noon, and now it's midnight. Beer, wine, vodka. But I seem clear-headed as I drive back to San Francisco; the food must have soaked it all up. My stomach, however, is distended, a football.

And Phil is not in, though he said he'd be home hours before me. I have no key: Matt is in New Jersey and Robert at his mother's, so I sit in the car becoming increasingly worried—arrested for drunk driving? Asleep somewhere, incapable because of the booze? Killed in a crash? One a.m.: I drive along Dolores, but I don't know the number of the house where he's feasting. I search—without success—for his car. Back to the flat. Two a.m. It looks as if I'll be out of doors all night. But Robert comes home (with a man) at 2.30: I can now get warm and sleep in a bed. Has he seen or heard anything of Phil? "Oh, he's OK," Robert tells me. "Been drinking, of course. He's taking a breath of fresh air—we were in a bar on Castro."

I feel very angry. How inconsiderate! A few minutes later he arrives, reeking of alcohol and grinning foolishly. Endless I'm sorrys and kisses I can't respond to. Then "I've brought someone back. Is it OK if he comes to bed with us?" We've not talked about three-ways, though we've said that when we're apart we have sex with other men. I'm astonished: I wouldn't have brought a guy home without discussing the matter first.

An Australian, Bruce—would you believe? I watch him take off his clothes. A well-built hunk, suntanned, with a broad, very hairy chest and a massive cock. Just looking at him I'm upright. Three-way kisses—deliciously erotic. Phil has drunk too much and can't get it hard; I climb over him to the Australian. "David doesn't seem to mind at all!" Phil says. Not only surprise in his voice—a certain plaintiveness. The Australian fucks him; I fuck the Australian. Afterwards, stroking each

[51]

other's cocks and gently kissing, our skins sticky with sweat, KY, sperm, I think what an international occasion this is— Vietnam, Australia and Britain all in one bed. Drifting towards sleep, it occurs to me that if our presidents and prime ministers allowed themselves to do this there might be no more wars . . . Ronald, Leonid, Maggie . . .

Often in the past I've bottled up annoyance with a lover, sulked for ages, and it ruined our sex life, ruined everything, left me finally furious with myself because it was so difficult to snap out of it. But on this occasion . . . my anger with Phil has completely disappeared.

SHOPPING DOWNTOWN, tea and cakes in a café on Balboa, in Ghirardelli Square to see Christmas lights switched on, a juggler entertaining a crowd: San Francisco street life, Thanksgiving weekend.

How beautiful he is.

WITH MATT AWAY AND ROBERT out most of the time—in South of Market bars or at his mother's or Candlestick watching the Forty-niners ball-game—we have the apartment to ourselves. Which is very nice; there's an extra warmth and intimacy between us as we cook dinner or lie on the sofa watching TV, a suggestion of what's to come when we have our own place in January. Yet I find I've missed Matt this long weekend; I enjoy coffee with him in the early morning, Saturdays and Sundays while Phil sleeps in late, swopping details of what we've each been doing the past few days. It's interesting to observe him and Robert in their home: I like to watch gay couples in the same space peaceably moving round one another, to speculate on why this picture was bought, which episode of their lives does that souvenir represent, and note who does what, enjoying the many significant differences between their life-styles and those of straight lovers, taking part in the easy conversations straights could never have. I want the same thing for myself; it's been a two-year absence.

Last November in Frankfurt I spent a few hours in the tiny flat Dieter and Fritz have shared for more than a decade. It was cluttered almost beyond belief with records and books and so many plants I thought I was inside a conservatory. Serious, gentle, kindly men. (With quite the largest feet I have ever seen.) Just watching them hurt. I wanted them to take me to bed: it didn't happen. I've no idea if they indulged in three-ways, or, if they did, whether they would have wanted to with me. But unfulfilled sexual desire was not the cause of the hurt: I had a lover at the time, but we never lived together.

A COLOSSAL STORM. Trees down everywhere: power-lines, telephone cables broken. Five cars at the university crushed by a eucalyptus. A DC7 on a runway at San Francisco airport is blown into the Bay; it sinks in mud. Snow on the roads through the sierras cuts us off from the world again. This winter is a freak, everyone says; rainfall, snowfall are four hundred per cent higher than average.

VIII

AN INTERVIEW in the *San Francisco Chronicle* with Edmund White, whose prose I much admire. One of the best of modern gay writers. He says he had sex with five hundred different men before he was sixteen, and some of it would be regarded as violent sex. I had it once before I was sixteen—in the lavatory at school, with a boy whose cock was so vast I could scarcely get my two little hands round it. And there was no violence: just a very satisfying mutual wank. I often wonder what happened to Richard Lee—I'd like to play with that phenomenon again, to make sure time and imagination haven't played me false. It was a *prodigy*!

I don't envy Edmund White the fact that he had four hundred and ninety-nine more men than I did. How did he manage, in his schedule, to eat, sleep, go out with friends, finish his homework, talk to his family, and do the ordinary things that occupy the days of everyone, adolescent or otherwise? He must have been a specialist in only one area of life, and therefore tedious— as Tesman in *Hedda Gabler*, whose only interest was the industries of medieval Brabant, is tedious.

I don't think I've had five hundred men in all the years since sixteen, though it's probably not far off that number. Some of that heaving and groaning bored me stiff—I mean unstiff. But there were times I've loved the marathon of ten hours or more in a bath-house.

Five hundred men before the age of sixteen! But those publishers of young adult fiction, who blench at a manuscript in which a sixteen-year-old has a few naughty thoughts—let alone does it—should take note: teenagers do fuck, some of them repeatedly, and sometimes with their own sex. I'm no longer interested in writing young adult fiction—it's the middle-class hypocrisy over matters sexual I can't stand.

[54]

But was it all pleasure, Ed?

MY MOTHER OCCASIONALLY writes to me. She will be eighty next week, and though she is very doddery now all her mental faculties are intact. I wish I could be close to her, share parts of my life as a straight son might with his mother. But my homosexuality is something she has never come to terms with—has never rejoiced at the pleasures and achievements of my gay existence, nor comforted me in its periods of trauma and misery. She's missed out on so much—the enjoyment she could have got from knowing my lovers, for example. Every night she prays I'll be cured. If she has to pray, why not ask that I'll have a rewarding, contented life?

I once asked if she would leave me in her will the portrait of my grandmother that hangs in her sitting-room. "I don't know that Momma would want to see what goes on in *your* house," she said. And "fight it, fight it," she told me. "It's evil. It only brings unhappiness." To her, in effect.

But her most recent letter is startling: she'd like to come out here for a holiday. I don't think she has changed her attitudes at all; it's because she's extremely impressed with a few pages I wrote to her last month, trying to offer her some kind of comfort for the grief she still feels about my father's death two years ago. She'd be very welcome. I could put away some of the visible evidence of gayness, I suppose; the porn calendar and the KY tube, the mug in the kitchen that has the words KISS ME, I'M GAY on its side. I wouldn't want to. And I'll be living with Phil and sharing a bed with him; and I won't refuse to entertain our friends—she would have to accept all that. Probably see me touch him or kiss him.

I will not pretend to be other than what I am for *anybody*. So I suppose she won't come.

THE SAN FRANCISCO BOARD OF SUPERVISORS (the city and county council) has given Scott Smith five thousand dollars because he was Harvey Milk's "dependant". (Harvey Milk was shot dead in his City Hall office in November 1978 by Dan White who, moments before, had killed the mayor, George Moscone.) This is the first time any city in the world has

[55]

decided that the gay partner of one of its employees who has died should be treated in the same way as a bereaved husband or wife. Applause, applause. Muted applause—there are some odd features to this case. Only one supervisor voted against when the board made its decision; he said that it had not been proved that Smith was really a dependant, and that if he was he should have been awarded the full amount of money usually given to such people—*fifty* thousand dollars. Milk and Smith ran a photographic shop on Castro; they were business partners—and *ex*-lovers. "Dependant", therefore, is possibly not a strictly accurate definition of Smith's status. But if the authorities choose to think it is, what right have they to conclude that a gay is worth ten times less, financially, than a straight?

Milk's lover, in fact, was a young man who committed suicide a short while before the killings: if he were alive, would the Board of Supervisors have given the money to him instead of Scott Smith?

The annual ceremony to commemorate the murders of Harvey Milk and George Moscone was held last Saturday. We intended to go, but forgot. Quite inexcusable. Several thousand gay men and women, in sombre mood, marched from Castro to City Hall, each one holding a lighted candle. There is still a great deal of anger about the assassinations and the preposterous trial of Dan White, who will be out of jail early in 1984. I wouldn't want to be in his shoes: there is almost nowhere in the world he can hide.

Castro's public events aren't all costume parades and celebrations, and it would be wrong if they were. Gay history is not exactly an uninterrupted chronicle of triumphs.

I'M WRITING A PIECE on Virginia Hamilton for my book of essays on children's authors: it's evening; Katya is on the other side of the fire, sipping vodka and gazing absently into the flames. Sarah appears, not drunk, but she's certainly been drinking. (Since lunch-time, she tells us. Brandy.) The reasons I had to leave—the *sole* reason, she repeats—is because I wouldn't go to bed with Harriet. So Harriet turned nasty.

I was right, then.

She has made a decision. Or at least a decision to make a decision. To leave Harriet. Katya looks at me, eyes like saucers.

The evening's programme is abandoned (Katya and I were going out to a restaurant) and I cook steak, broccoli, tomatoes and mushrooms for the three of us. We drink till gone midnight. Does she want to talk to Katya in private? "No! If I'm going to talk to anyone, it will be to *you*."

Me? *Why*?

She sobers up gradually, and we talk of other things—the university, books, politics. But keep returning to the one subject of interest—the breakdown of her relationship with Harriet. What do I do, she asks. Where do I begin? Resign from the university? Go back east? I was a social being once, she says. Now I'm not. And what chance is there of any relationship enduring? Name one you know of that really works. We do, but she dismisses them all. There's a mild sort of violence in her tonight, turned in on herself because, I imagine, Harriet knows how to deflect her aggression. "How was Thanksgiving?" I ask. She ate two hot dogs and spent all day in her room.

Eventually she disappears into the night.

"Well . . ." Katya and I say to each other.

IN CONTRAST: PHIL IN LOS GATOS. Walking in the mountains, dancing at Los Desperados, dinner at Cats, which, we learn, was a brothel in the nineteenth century *and* outside its doors are two huge stone cats. So both theories concerning the origin of the name "Los Gatos" are correct. It's now a pleasant enough steak-house with country and western music. Saturday we drive over the mountains to San Gregorio: a day of bright sunshine and vivid fall leaves. A rushing ocean sweeping across smooth sand. No one else here. Back to Katya's for a dinner party: a log fire, and her children have come to decorate the house for Christmas. A tree that touches the ceiling: coloured lights, tinsel.

There will be a good Christmas in this place. But for Sarah and Harriet?

WE ARE SO RURAL that deer sometimes stray into the garden. This afternoon three of them, their movements elegant and precise as dancers, grazed for a while on the lawn. Our cat, Robert Redford, stalked them—very stealthily, flattened to the ground—then hid, or hoped he hid, behind a bush. That means his body was invisible, but he hadn't the sense to conceal his face; or curiosity was perhaps too strong. One of the deer noticed, stared for a while, then delicately stepped towards him, horns lowered. A long, long stillness. Then deer and cat rubbed noses, licked each other, and kissed.

THE VIEWS FROM KATYA'S: mountain soaring behind mountain. Shrouded in fog today, but majestic in a red sunrise, a gold dusk. Evenings, the lights of downtown San José in the distance, and the Santa Clara peaks beyond are pink bruises.

THE BOARD OF SUPERVISORS has proposed a new law to give the unmarried the same rights enjoyed by married couples: health insurance for the partner, hospital and jail visits, pensions for the bereaved. (The 1980 census showed that San Francisco has more unmarried people in its population than any other city in the United States.) Mayor Feinstein has vetoed the idea, much to the annoyance of the gay community, who would obviously be the principal beneficiaries. Gay San Francisco, after the Milk–Moscone assassinations, helped to vote her in and they have the muscle to vote her out. But all the analysts in the newspapers and on TV say that she probably doesn't care, may even be glad to dissociate herself from Castro: she's after higher things—the Democrat vice-presidential nomination. Gays are angry. Five hundred people stood outside City Hall for hours last night, shouting "Dump Feinstein!"

(They didn't. In November 1983 she was re-elected with an overwhelming majority. As Hilaire Belloc said:

> *"And always keep a-hold of nurse*
> *For fear of finding something worse."*)

GLORIA IS THE CURRENT NUMBER ONE. A great record, and every disco is playing it non-stop. I first heard it a year ago in Paris, at Le Palace, dancing with Andy. Now I dance to it in

San Francisco with Phil. The changes a year brings: all flux. Good.

AVRIL WALKING TOWARDS ME a long way off down an endless corridor. Tall thin women in billowing skirts are like Christmas trees.

An end-of-semester grade-athon. Thirteen of us shut up on a Saturday in a room without windows from 8 a.m. till 4 p.m. "Now you have the full experience of America's Puritan heritage," says the Department chairman, meeting me on a pedestrian crossing at 7.30 in raw cold fog. Every script has to be marked twice. By three o'clock, after reading one hundred and twenty compositions on whether people work to obtain necessities or luxuries, I'm boss-eyed and mind-blown. Our periodic discussions on standardizing marks are serious, indeed meticulous. I feel totally remote from real life: six thousand miles from roots, listening to grading instructions in Americanese. What am I doing here?

IN THE RESTAURANT AT EMPORIUM, one of San Francisco's largest department stores, eating a chicken salad. Phil is in Macy's buying my Christmas present; I have time to relax after a hectic morning in shops. Above me is the roof, a glass dome, Victorian Monumental; a gigantic Christmas tree (surely the city's biggest) fills up the space beneath—soars up so high its top is almost invisible. Gaggles of old ladies drinking coffee and genteelly toying with expensive sticky cakes: female old ladies of a breed almost extinct, rich, in furs and hats and jewellery and garish make-up. On a balcony some way off an orchestra plays; the music sounds Jewish. It's all a bit like Chekhov.

This superb city.

I came to San Francisco in the 1980s as Herr Issyvoo came to Berlin in the 1930s: because it has the reputation of being the wickedest place on earth, a phoenix Sodom; me, as he, an iron filing to a magnet. This diary should be one long hymn of praise to its beauty, the fascination of its streets, the diversity of its life-styles, the joys of its fleshly pleasures, the satisfactions of sex with its men. As on so many previous occasions here, I feel enchanted, under a spell: fulfilled and happy.

ON A PLANE, LONDON-BOUND. Eleven hours of flying. I knew beforehand there would be the ache of absence, but I was not prepared for this much.

San Francisco. Phil. I love you both.

Four weeks, Christmas, will soon pass.

IX

AND SOON PASSED THEY HAVE. California in a cool wet January, as green as England.

The month away I felt neither here, nor there, but suspended in mid-Atlantic, a foot in both—camps? Ulrich, totally bound to making money in his restaurant; for him, it is not the time of life to have lovers: as good in bed, though, as he always was. My mother at eighty, confused and depressed: relationships falling apart, divorces looming. Snow on the hills outside Exeter. My house is being well looked after by Andy. Parties, drinks, dinner parties with friends: Christmas. At a disco I win a prize for the most unusual costume; I went as a San Francisco hustler, in shorts, white socks, Stetson, the words WANNA FUCK? in queenly pink on a white tee-shirt. London: digging money out of publishers whose payments are long overdue, who are taking advantage of my being six thousand miles off.

Lengthy inter-continental calls. "Come home, baby!" he says. "Come h-o-o-o-me!" I reassure him I will, but I don't think he'll believe it till he sees me at the airport. San Antonio, El Paso, New Orleans, Memphis—his long car-ride to spend Christmas in Kentucky is punctuated with these conversations from motel bedrooms, and when he returns to San Francisco *my* phone bill mounts with the quickness of a dial on a petrol pump.

An accidental meeting at the hairdresser's with Gene Kemp: side by side, looking utterly grotesque—wreathed in towels, our hair sticky and hideous, full of dye, standing up all ends as the girls restore the black we were born with. Gene, another Exeter writer, won the Carnegie Medal for *The Turbulent Term of Tyke Tyler* the year before I was given it for *The Exeter Blitz*. The two of us, winners of this supposedly most prestigious of children's book awards, in a provincial beauty salon looking like Guy Fawkes dummies, discuss the unprintable and slanderous gossip of the kiddie lit. world. Gossip of the gay lit. world—in London with Peter—had been, the previous week, more elegant; over China tea and Peter's favourite brandy-snaps. And almost fit to print.

To San Francisco, to Phil, making love, boxes of chocolates, wine, pizza at the Sausage Factory, and jet lag. Jet lag gives me bad dreams. I wake and he stirs, holds me, whispers "You OK?" and I sleep again, profoundly, without dreams. Apartment hunting. We find it, eventually; on Douglass, the ground floor of a little Victorian—bedroom, bathroom, kitchen, living-room—a mile east of Castro, not far from the brunch restaurants and the Habitat shops on 24th. The house is owned by Brenda and Valerie, two gay women who live upstairs. Moving in tomorrow. If all this is my heart's desire, I'd better learn how to live with it.

THE LEARNING PROCESS BEGINS AT ONCE. For him, I guess, there is my energy and impatience; for me, adapting to a life-style that seems peculiarly boxed in. He's restricted himself to a permitted field of activities I find unnecessarily narrow. His week-days consist of his work, the journey to work, the slow routine of the bathroom between 6 and 8 a.m., and in the evening, as soon as we've eaten, he's ready for bed, unless he has laundry to sort out. I have never met anyone who takes so long in the bathroom or who's so fussy about his clothes. Towels are put in the wash after they've been used twice. Do I really want, I ask myself in a moment of exasperation, to live with a man whose chief concerns in his free time are washing his hair and ironing his shirts? What would I like that time to be devoted to? Well, certainly not discos every night of the week; I'm happy to stay indoors—to talk, watch TV, listen to music, read. Go out for a drink on occasion, a walk. So I'm not exactly losing out on anything important. It's what has happened inside *him* that bothers me; this excessively thin range. A result of the tragic years before he arrived in America?

I decide eventually that it's not my business; his bathroom hours and his dirty underwear aren't really of import to me. A weekend packed with shared activity—calling on Robert and Matt, Kevin and Ivor to dinner, the San Francisco Ballet's fiftieth anniversary gala at the Opera House, dinner with Janos, dancing at the I-Beam, and still time enough to potter about the flat, to make love in the afternoons—and my judgements on how he fills up his days seem trivial, bossy.

A STEREOTYPICAL GAY SCENE that amuses me: we're shifting the furniture about in the living-room, getting it just right—should that plant be moved a centimetre, the clock go on the bookcase, the picture be lowered an inch?—when a quartet of *enormous* women (thighs and buttocks of vast size) brandishing hammers and crow-bars, begin to attack the wooden staircase that leads up to Brenda and Valerie's front door. The planks are half-rotten; this is the demolition and repair gang. In no time at all wood is hurtling in every direction. Phil gently taps a nail into the wall, hangs a picture, and we fear for the safety of our windows, ourselves. I go outside and talk with the women; we joke about gay guys delicately arranging their ornaments while the lesbians roll up their sleeves and do some proper real-men-don't-eat-quiche work. At which point a flying plank spears me in the leg and I spill the beer I'm drinking. Profuse apologies, author-queen-damaged-by-dyke-construction-worker jokes, and a great deal of laughter.

THE BRAQUE EXHIBITION, a major retrospective, at the Palace of the Legion of Honor: the cool subtle colours of all those interiors and still lives, the quality of absolute calm at their centres. I think again of Sibelius—"the landscape of the mind"—and I feel satisfied, rewarded, as I did listening to Britten in the Presbyterian church last December: the wintry urban Sunday afternoon becomes worthwhile.

We look at the rest of the museum. There is among the Monets here a riverside scene with trees in full leaf: one of the great Monets, as fine as anything in Europe.

KEVIN, AT WHOSE HOUSE PHIL spent Thanksgiving, is beaten up and robbed where Dolores crosses 18th. A gentle harmless man—a priest. But Dolores and 18th is a few blocks from the Mission; it's the frontier between Gayville and Chicanotown. Gays have been attacked here before, particularly in or close to the a.y.o.r. ill-lit park on the corner.

I've been in the Mission two or three times at night—my local cash-point is Mission and 29th. It's a creepy, sinister district, its poverty all the more obvious from being so near Castro's painted middle-class Victorians, but as far east as 29th it's relatively safe. Eighteenth, however, is another matter. I'd not feel safe on foot, alone after dark, on 18th north of Sanchez or Church—by Dolores it's definitely a no-go area.

Matt tells me Robert was leaving a bar on Folsom late one night and a car drove straight into him. It was a deliberate attempt to murder: a lot of sick people haunt South of Market. Robert was thrown, by the impact, over the car roof and on to the street, miraculously unhurt except for severe bruising. The driver accelerated off into the distance.

Kevin was mugged on a previous occasion, outside a bar on Harrison. But the assailant was caught this time; Kevin pinned him to the ground while Robert phoned the cops.

These stories bring back the old unease, astonishment that such violence simmers just under the surface of this city, the fear that one day I could be the victim. And if the victim is selected because he's vulnerable, then how much less macho Phil looks than me.

HARRIET AND SARAH spent Christmas together in Mexico. But Katya has no idea of what sort of Christmas it was; the silence from up the road is deafening. I miss Los Gatos, the view from Katya's windows of garden, trees and mountains. The rural quiet, the deer. "You must think of this house as your second home," she says. She was worried, after my move to San Francisco, that she'd see little of me. But I'm there two or three times a week. Talking and drinking with her, our bridge games with Janos and Tim, are an important part of my existence.

Much as I like the flat I'll get bothered when the weather is warmer. There isn't a place I can sunbathe and write out of doors. It sounds trivial, but I know it will be a major problem. I'll write, perhaps, in Katya's garden; but it's more than fifty miles off. I can't do that every day of the week.

Yet there is such pleasure, the rare mild hours we have this February, in walking about San Francisco. Always new corners, new vistas that please. Acacias in full bloom are fountains of dazzling yellow; daffodils, camelias, red hot pokers, montbretia, lilies blossom in Castro front gardens; oleander is already in bud outside the window of our apartment. Used to the place as I am, I still look at houses as a tourist: a Hammer-film folly on Douglass and 20th, an elaborate pink-and-white delicacy on Eureka, a sundae quite literally all colours of the rainbow on Clipper. The care, the attention to detail on every intricately patterned façade! The turrets, gables, friezes, frescoes, cornices, mouldings, pom-poms, curlicues and fol-de-rols all of wood—nowhere else have I seen the skill of the wood-carver so magnificently displayed as it is in San Francisco. With an unlimited supply of wood and a city to construct, the Victorian builders could have made as much of a desert as they did with stone and brick in any British suburb; but here they took pride in creating, with almost every house, a work of art.

Mild days, I said; but there has been lashing rain and ferocious wind. Streets flooded, avalanches of mud, houses battered to bits by gigantic waves or falling from crumbled cliffs into the sea. Blizzards: Katya, driving for only two hours into the sierras, has to buy chains to get herself home. A gust of wind rips out the windows of 18th's post office—the mass of splintered glass on the street is as if a bomb has exploded. No injuries are reported, but any passing queen would have had his beauty ruined for life.

JANOS HAS WRITTEN TO HIS PARENTS, telling them that he is gay. A long, carefully considered letter, accompanied by a copy of *Now That You Know* (a book by Betty Fairchild and Nancy Hayward that aims to help parents develop positive attitudes to their gay children). We discussed, in great detail before he sent it, the pros and cons. His lover, Jim, is as important to him as his brothers' girl-friends are to his brothers; the lies and the pretence disgust him; and if he goes home to Seattle in April to his sister's wedding, he wants Jim to be with him.

Phil has organized his car-pool so I can have his car for my days at the university: mine uses so much more gas. I won't do it all the time—it's a round trip of a hundred miles to San José and back; I don't think *I* should wear out his car.

Kindness, consideration, thinking of *my* needs.

Janos says the way to find out whether your cock is of reasonable size is to sit on the lavatory and see if it dangles into the water. (Water in an American loo-pan comes up higher than in the British equivalent.) Phil and I both pass the test . . . His looks almost semi-submerged . . .

SAN FRANCISCO BALLET fiftieth anniversary gala performance, razzmatazz at the Opera House: flowers, balloons, fireworks. Not the most marvellous dance I've ever seen—too itsy-bitsy—but great entertainment. Gene Kelly in the flesh!

The *pas de deux* from Act Two of *Swan Lake*, the epitome of classical ballet: moonlight, white tutus superior to their counterparts in *Giselle* and *Les Sylphides*. Mainly, I guess, because of the music. There are other composers who were gay or bisexual, but only with Tchaikovsky and Britten is their homosexuality an obvious, integral part of their work, its *raison d'être*. *Les Illuminations* is not just love songs; it's gay love songs. *Billy Budd* is a gay opera. The *Swan Lake pas de deux* is adolescent yearning: the separateness of the violin and the cello solos—two boys longing to touch—love that's doomed. It's ironic that the straight public find such comfort and consolation in Tchaikovsky; his music is always an expression of his unhappy, unfulfilled gay self, yet he speaks to everyone. It's a reflection of the world's bewilderment, frustration and misery.

The movements and the gestures of the dancers in the *pas de deux* are symbols of love-making; how he uses his height to shield her, draw her to himself, is as I lie against Phil, or Phil on his back, my arms round him, protecting what I see as his vulnerability.

BRIDGE WITH TIM AT ROBERT AND MATT'S. But Matt is ill; a friend of his, Lee, plays instead. Lee is gorgeous. Big male man with enormous arm muscles, hairy chest and strikingly handsome face. I'd love to go to bed with him. To be fucked. I wonder if I can organize a three-way, but Phil is not enthusiastic. I drink instead, and eventually play my cards very badly. Tim and I go down seven hundred points on one hand. Later, I screw Phil, imagining I'm Lee. It's good . . .

X

M. E. KERR'S *GENTLEHANDS*, a novel for young adults, is very disturbing. The sixteen-year-old narrator, Buddy Boyle, quarrels with his parents and moves in with his German grandfather, Herr Trenker, a kind, thoughtful, sweet man, who gives the boy all the material and emotional comfort he lacks at home. At a party Buddy meets a Jewish journalist whose sister was tortured to death by the Nazis; his mission in life is to track down and expose her killer who is responsible for slaughtering thousands of other Jews. In a newspaper article he names Buddy's grandfather as the wanted man, and, we find, Herr Trenker *is* the Nazi war criminal . . .

The story suddenly stops at this point, leaving the reader confused, indeed outraged. What is the author's intention? To make us realize that Nazi murderers loved their families? To make us feel compassion for such people? If a novel for children or teenagers has to differ from a novel for adults, it is in this: the author should avoid leaving his audience in total depression or despair. Though books for the young don't need to end happily every time, they ought to have some ray of hope. Of course the teenager has to learn about death, the fact that the world is messy and corrupt; but the final sentence of *Gentlehands* shows the author running away—"I just want to leave everything about that summer behind me." I feel just as Buddy Boyle does: I want to leave everything about this novel behind me.

I spent a rather miserable two weeks in Germany with Ulrich. I'm sure—and he even admitted it—that had he been alive in 1933 he'd have joined the Nazi Party. Blond, blue-eyed, obsessed with making money and intensely disliking Jews, he'd have made a splendid Hitler youth. I cannot begin to understand why anyone should dislike a whole race, a skin colour—a sexual preference. A threat to status, to certainties?

I have at times experienced, during sex, inflicting pain or having pain inflicted on me—a similar thrill to that of Nazis torturing Jews? No. I and my partners agreed to do what we did, and we enjoyed it; the Jews did not.

HASSLES WITH THE INSURANCE COMPANY over the payment of my hospital bills of last October. Letters back and forth, time wasted . . . Our socialist system is the better.

MAYBE IT'S A PROBLEM ONLY GAYS HAVE, and only a few of them at that: it took me most of a decade to discover I was the one who needed to fuck. Why so long? The image one has of oneself? Conditioning? Thinking my body wasn't male enough? I don't know. My sexual desires changed when I started going regularly to a gym; when my muscles began to look like those on the bodies I fancied, I ceased to fancy them and I turned to fucking slim, youthful men. I love it still. No post-coital *tristesse*.

PHIL'S CAR WAS VANDALIZED LAST NIGHT. Someone smashed the rear window, not just by throwing a stone or a bottle; it was methodically crushed into little bits and the frame yanked out. It must have taken some time, but, though the car was parked outside the house, we didn't hear anything. Nor did Brenda and Valerie. Phil's insurance policy says that he has to pay the first hundred dollars of any damage.

Kids, or drunks: an isolated incident, we hope. Someone doesn't like gays? Possible. Not probable. Easy to get uneasy in this city, even on respectable Douglass.

I wake at 3.30 and think I hear footsteps, then someone out the back, knocking dustbin lids.

Easy to get uneasy . . .

JANOS'S MOTHER WRITES. It's as good a letter as he could wish for. I don't understand, she says; perhaps I'll never understand. But I love you. Nothing has changed. And your brothers and your sister, who've all seen your letter, say they love you too; you're the same old Janos. One awkward paragraph—your father is finding it difficult. And a lot of omissions; it's very carefully worded. Janos has mentioned Jim, but Jim is not referred to.

It's a good start, however. He's elated.

REMARKABLE QUANTITIES OF DOG SHIT on the side-walks of Castro. San Francisco is so unpolluted; its buildings are the cleanest in the world. But the pavements are as dirty as those of Amsterdam.

MR AND MRS JANCZSO SEND JANOS A VALENTINE. I think it's been deliberately chosen—

> *A son is a joy every day the year through,*
> *That is if he's someone exactly like you!*
> *Someone who's dear in his own special way.*

(Which doesn't rhyme with "Because he is gay" though that, I suppose, could be inferred.) I guess they imagine his homosexuality a severe handicap, as if he had an incurable disease; that it has made him neurotic, and he therefore needs extra love and help.

Valentine's Day is taken much more seriously, perhaps I mean commercially, than in Britain. Not only the cards on sale, but displays in shops are geared to the event, with pink drapes, cardboard hearts and Cupids, plastic bows and arrows. More husbands, wives, lovers exchange presents—chocolates or flowers—than at home. I like this, a day to celebrate relationships. I also like the card in a Castro gift shop showing a naked man (back view) with a butch winged Cupid firing an arrow up his bum, and the card with a naked man (front view), his balls and cock covered with a huge red heart held by another man's hand protruding between his legs. The gay tat vendors don't miss a thing; I nearly said trick.

TO THE SAN FRANCISCO BALLET AGAIN: Caniparoli's *Chansons de Shéhérezade*, Smuin's *Stravinsky Piano Pieces*, Balanchine's *Western Symphony* and Kylian's *Forgotten Land*. This last is danced to Britten's *Sinfonia da Requiem*. Though the choreography throughout clearly stems from the score (I dislike dance which seems to ride roughshod over the music—it gives me the feeling any old sequence of chords will do), I wondered if it was a wise choice; the *Sinfonia da Requiem* is so compelling and complex that I often found I was just listening to the music and ignoring the dancers. Seeing *Death in Venice* at Covent Garden a few years ago produced a similar response—should I concentrate on the sets, the singing, the action, or the fascinating sounds the orchestra was producing? I just couldn't take it all in at once.

The *Sinfonia da Requiem* is Britten's only major work for the orchestra, but the mastery is absolute; it's as rich as Berlioz. The nervous energy, the quick clusters of notes, the clashing cross-rhythms command attention; and I love the clarity—you can always hear everything that's going on. There is a lot of self-pity in Britten's music, especially in the operas—the mourning for innocence, the damaged child, the damaged man or woman, Grimes, Lucretia, Albert Herring, Billy, Miles, Aschenbach, himself?—but it's not so heart-on-sleeve as in Tchaikovsky. Is it with both composers that being gay is a wound like that of Philoctetes: a sore that's incurable? I wish I knew more about Britten's life. The biographies skate over his homosexuality, pretending it's unimportant when in fact it seems to be there in nearly every note he put down on a stave. Britten must have had a happier existence than Tchaikovsky; the *Purcell Variations*, *Noye's Fludde*, the *Nocturne*, *Les Illuminations*, the *Serenade* suggest that he did. But they're rare moments: his music on the whole is dark and tragic. Coming out would not have been easy for a man born in 1913, yet his relationship with Peter Pears was an open secret and it lasted all his adult life. So—what was his problem?

The composer of *Chansons de Shéhérezade* is Ravel, and the choreographer perhaps found Ravel's homosexuality reflected in his music. The dancers were two men and a woman: one sequence was danced by the men, erotic and tender, and another closed with the men kneeling, arms round each other, kissing. I wish there was more overtly gay classical ballet. Male dancers are frequently homosexual, but everything, from *Swan Lake* to *Pineapple Poll*, pretends to be as strait-laced as a tutu.

NOT IN A GOOD MOOD. It's pouring with rain; my sweaters disappear from the laundrette, and my attempt to join the San Francisco public library is a failure. Apart from the usual ID red tape, the library clerk wants a deposit of eleven dollars. I've never heard of anything so ridiculous, and I say so. Eleven dollars to borrow—for instance—books I've written myself. The library at Los Gatos wanted neither identification nor money. And while I'm feeling bad-tempered, I might as well announce that I think Scott Smith's attempt to get more money out of the supervisors because he was Harvey Milk's lover should also end in failure. It was established in court yesterday that they were not lovers during the last two years of Milk's life. If we want to have the same legal rights as married straights, we should draw attention to more credible relationships. What about it, Peter Pears?

Did I say I wanted this diary to be "a hymn of praise to the beauty of San Francisco"?

My sweaters mysteriously surface in the laundry of a New Wave blond who works in the local ethnic bakery; I can always use Phil's library ticket; and the rain cannot last for ever. So I'll on with my hymn of praise . . .

WE DRIVE NORTH OVER THE GOLDEN GATE, through Marin County to Russian River. Warm spring sunlight, emerald fields, acacias like yellow bonfires. The river is brown, in full flood, surging through pine woods; I half-expect to see logs and lumberjacks. I fuck Phil against a tree, and we've only just got our jeans back on when a boy of about sixteen emerges from the bushes to tell us we're trespassing on private property. I hope he enjoyed what he must have observed.

Dinner parties every night this public holiday weekend. Kevin, Tim, Janos, Dennis and Paul, Nils and Alan here; a phalanx of Asiatic professors at Katya's. She has gossip about Sarah and Harriet. Sarah has left and is staying with the chairman of our department and his wife. I could wish to be a fly on that particular wall . . . Harriet, alone and lonely, calls Katya after months of silence to see if she'll go to a movie. Katya says no.

We drink excessively, Friday night, Saturday night, Sunday

night. Mardi Gras disco at Los Desperados, dancing with Phil. I wonder how we've got there (though I was at the wheel, I have no recollection of the drive) and I take *all* my clothes off on the dance floor. *Drunk* . . .

READING A LIFE OF TCHAIKOVSKY. He and Brahms once found each other staying at the same hotel—what on earth, I wonder, did they talk about? Brahms disliked Tchaikovsky's music: "His seams show." Tchaikovsky had a great admiration for Berlioz. I've always thought the *Fantastique* the matrix of the *Pathétique*—similar adolescent yearning, frenzy, drawing the listener into a spell he at first wants to reject; the second movement the best waltz Tchaikovsky did not write.

A LETTER FROM SPEARFISH. "A gay person could die of loneliness in a small town. I am so sick of going to a cinema on my nights off. I want to feel I belong somewhere." He'll be working in Las Vegas for the summer, then he will move, permanently, to Dallas. "I so wanted to meet you," he says, "but I guess life doesn't always take the direction we wish for." He encloses a recent photograph; older, his face a little more filled out than when he was a teenager. We'll meet before I return to England, of that I'm determined. For one night at least. As I'd like an hour with the blond who lives on Collingwood. I've never spoken to this guy and I don't know who he is, but I sometimes pass his house on my walks round the city. Slim, butch, long curly hair—like Dan. He sits at his window and we stare at each other; last week we got so far as a mutual friendly wave. If only he'd invite me in . . .

Phil says I should ask Gary to visit when he's en route for Las Vegas. It would be crazy, he adds, never to meet him. If he really does look like his photographs, I answer, I'd want him in bed. Phil says that's OK. So I write to Gary and suggest he comes.

WE'RE PULLING UP AT THE LIGHTS where 18th crosses, and a bearded nun dashes up to the car and hands me a poster advertising a disco. "Slow down," I say. "We can gaze at the men as we drive past." They've all crawled out of the woodwork

[72]

this warm, sunny Saturday afternoon. I glance at Phil, who is looking into the mirror and fussing with his hair. Phil is the only gay in the world who'd drive through Castro watching his own reflection.

I still find his obsessive concern with his appearance, the hours in the bathroom, the perpetual dithering, hard to adjust to. His life is slipping by, and he does nothing. We're complete opposites. "Opposition is true friendship," Blake said.

MISSING—A GREAT FILM. Uplifting, harrowing.

A performance of Mahler's ninth. Ecstasy always out of reach or lost in the past; a man at the point of death trying to make sense of his life. Too long, too bitter-sweet—though it grips me, moves me.

Joe Orton acted by Americans is a strange experience. *Loot*'s anarchy should be universal in its appeal, but it's an obstinately British piece of theatre: the Wilde influence makes it untransferable, too reminiscent of cut-glass voices, of Lady Bracknell *et al*. A second-rate production, slipshod and over the top, none of the accents right, the gay theme skimmed over; but I enjoy it nonetheless—it's such a good play.

Phil, and most of the audience, are bewildered. They can't see it as funny.

XI

I DON'T THINK I WOULD SAY that since I came out, since I've
led a completely homosexual existence, I've always been
happier—apart from the pleasures of thousands of orgasms—
than when I thought I could be heterosexual. There have been
tragic moments. Heart-breaking experiences. But I'm a damn
sight more comfortable inside my own skin.

Coming out freed me as a writer too. If I can go on finding
beautiful male bodies, and if I can write all the books that I have
inside me, I'll not gaze back with Mahler's bitter-sweetness, but
think, yes, it was worthwhile, all of it.

So far so good.

PHIL, IN A CLINGING MOOD, worries that I am leaving him at
the end of my California year. He'll never get over it, he says.
He will, of course. And each succeeding time become a little bit
tougher, more immune to hurt, find eventually that the only
security is in himself.

He is so vulnerable. But the most attractive vulnerability is a
man undressing.

WITH PHIL, ROBERT AND MATT to the Kezar Pavilion to see
the gay basketball team play the University of California, a
jamboree put on by the Sisters of Perpetual Indulgence. The
Sisters, in full regalia except for very brief black and white
mini-skirts, are cheerleaders and sweepers-up: scampering
about the gym, their wimples flying, they look like busy
spiders. The Gay Men's Chorus, the San Francisco Gay Freedom Day Marching Band and Twirling Corps, the Oakland
Raw-rahs: there's more entertainment than basketball. We
watch a new nun being invested. What qualifications are needed
to become a Sister, what is the purpose of the organization? To

bring some colour to our lives, I suppose. They stage-manage gay functions, perform cabaret; they're political—in the city council elections last November Sister Boom-Boom got twenty-three thousand votes—and they are noticed, get gay life noticed.

Our team is as macho a collection of clones as I've ever seen, with bulging arm muscles, billowing hairy chests and thighs like sequoia trees. University, in comparison, are a bunch of anaemic wimps. But we lose. We can do anything except toss the ball into the net—a major disability.

Afterwards a disco, our second in two days. (Last night we were at the I-Beam.) Though we're not tired, and it's good to dance on the great space of a gymnasium floor, it quickly becomes less than exciting because of the music—dreadful mind-banging stuff, all at the wrong speed. Everybody in the Peninsula, on the subject of disco, says the same thing—no dj now plays music that is fun to dance to, that you're able to dance to. More and more the records are what *he* likes, not what the patrons want. Just as in England, I tell them. One could leave, of course; hundreds of people on this occasion did leave, rapidly. But often one stays, hoping the music will improve. It rarely does. Whatever happened to the Bee Gees, to Diana Ross?

I get talking to some of the nuns, who all agree that the music is *awful*. It's by Sister Freeda Peoples, they tell me, the disc jockey from Castro Station, and they won't ask her (him) to do it again.

THE GUY BEHIND THE COUNTER in our nearest grocery store says I must stop wearing shorts; my legs turn him on too much. I quite fancy him, and though I'm not really in the mood we suck each other off behind the freezer, standing up. He has a good body and a massive cock.

Why does one do this? Because it's there, I suppose, as mountaineers say of Everest. I didn't need this man particularly; it didn't matter if I had him or not. I guess I wanted to fulfil the expectations implied in the compliment about my legs; I had to show him he wasn't wrong. And it would be absurd not to accept the offer an attractive man makes by removing his clothes for you.

[75]

Phil is not pleased. "You have very bad taste," he says. "That guy is loud, too familiar, and ugly."

"Is this wanting to do something yourself, but if your lover does it that's another story?"

"OK, fair enough. But I can't have a relationship with someone who's doing that all the time."

"I'm not doing 'that' all the time!" I point out, truthfully. "And I can't have a relationship with someone who has double standards. Who won't allow me to do what I like with my own body."

"We're animals. That's what's wrong with gay life. We look at men in the street and assess them solely on whether we want their cocks. It's dehumanizing!"

"Next time I won't tell you. Which is bad—it makes it seem more important than it is."

The day after, he says he's sorry and that he can't justifiably complain about me doing what, if the opportunity arises, he does himself. I decide to dismiss the whole thing as a bout of insecurity. I hope it's not more than that. If it is, our relationship won't last.

AT MASONIC HALL WITH JIM AND JANOS for an evening of operatic arias and duets. Lee comes with us. He's as hairy and hunky as ever. I flirt with him; he flirts with Phil—but nothing results.

Masonic Hall, an impressive, comfortable auditorium, is used for recitals and chamber music. San Francisco, whose population is about the same as Bristol's, has this and a full-size concert hall, a symphony orchestra, an opera house with an opera company that is world-famous, several theatres, an excellent ballet troupe (they are having their own theatre built at the moment), and three art galleries. It puts most cities—in *any* country—to shame.

THE QUEEN (YES, ELIZABETH II) visits San Francisco in appalling weather—non-stop rain, gales, mud-slides, houses falling into the ocean, whole towns flooded, thousands homeless. In England we never really think it will freeze for days on end, and in consequence have instant chaos when half an inch of snow falls; so Californians assume it cannot rain for long. They build ramshackle houses on precarious hillsides or at the edge of the sea, then marvel that they collapse; they construct roads with little or no camber so water cannot drain off them, then they're horrified by the bad driving conditions. As soon as the Queen departs, the sun comes out. It's warm, and suddenly I'm aware again of the mountains, of flower scents, of trees and shrubs in bloom—stretches of magnolia, oleander, japonica, almond, blue coeanothus.

The Queen has a mixed Press. Several editorials thunder away on the extravagance and frivolity of the monarchical system; some even sound as if the War of Independence had never finished. Lots of demonstrations, particularly by the Irish. Katya celebrates her fiftieth birthday at a "Free Ireland Now" rally. No American I've talked to has any idea of the complexities of the crisis in Ulster. It's seen as a simple colonial problem, wicked Brits and enslaved Paddies. Nothing I propound, despite my impeccable Southern Irish origins, can shift them; Dermot Keogh, who comes from the University of Cork and is, like me, a visiting professor at San José, has the same difficulty. We are in a minority of two.

PHIL AND I JOIN KATYA and her family for a picnic in Golden Gate Park. While we're eating we hear gunshots, and later, looking at the news on TV, we learn that a seventeen-year-old girl who was sitting in the rose garden has been shot dead by a maniac.

ST PATRICK'S DAY and I see a sticker in a window—VICTORY TO THE IRA. A black on 18th is wearing a green wig.

CLICHÉS IN STUDENT ASSIGNMENTS: America is the Great Melting-Pot, the Land of Opportunity, the Land of Freedom. Unemployment, discrimination, prejudice, limits on freedom exist here as much as they do in any other democracy. An opinion poll published today says Americans are the most satisfied, the proudest, the most God-fearing people on earth. For satisfied one could read self-satisfied; for proud, insular; for God-fearing, hypocritical. There is less evident chauvinism

[77]

than in France, but many Americans cannot conceive of anything interesting or important outside the United States. News coverage on radio and TV, in the papers, is quite astonishingly inward-looking, except for the focus on Israel—there is always something on Israel: the fifty-first state. Stories from Britain consist of little more than what the Queen is wearing. Of the twenty-eight pages of news in this Sunday's *Examiner and Chronicle* two are devoted to the "World." Three items in all, in between the adverts—American journalists kidnapped in El Salvador; Reagan's views on the presence of Israeli troops in Lebanon; and the only topic that is totally unAmerican, and apparently worth printing, is the weakness of the franc since the socialists came to power in France. Perfect way to breed a nation of the uninformed.

Americans don't see that their medical system is indefensible by any civilized standards, that their urban life is more violent, their banking in some ways more antiquated, their telephone system less efficient than that of some European countries; that they aren't God's chosen people. And I was not happy to be asked at the End-up disco this weekend for proof of my identity. I had nothing with me to say who I was and had to come home to get my driving licence. ID is a reminder that America imposes some restrictions on "freedom" that we would not tolerate in Britain.

There are innumerable compensations, of course. Politeness, openness, warmth: you can arrive at the most remote part of anywhere at 3 a.m. and find coffee, a meal, gasoline, a bed. Cheap booze, cigarettes, petrol; good restaurants and reasonable licensing laws; the weather (in California, but not this week); the landscape; the leafy suburbs (even San José is preferable to Ealing); the space. The baths.

And San Francisco.

THE GAY PAPERS AT THE MOMENT are almost entirely concerned with AIDS. New theories—it's caused by parasites; its incubation period is eighteen months to two years. The death toll is rising, and some people have died quite horribly. More and more people are more and more worried. Mythology grows too. An AIDS sufferer was recently refused admission to a Castro restaurant—as if the disease were infectious like the common cold, or a lethal germ one could catch from an unwashed plate.

Yet I couldn't resist the temptation to go to the Watergarden on Good Friday. Not much action, although it's a holiday for some workers; the scare is emptying the bath-houses. I have to make do with being sucked off by a man I really didn't find attractive at all.

JANOS'S MOTHER'S BIRTHDAY. A lengthy phone call, the dreaded subject not aired. One of his brothers had said to him earlier in the week that Mom didn't really want to talk at the moment, didn't know what to say to her eldest son. She'll cope, I guess, if the subject is never mentioned again, if he returns to Seattle always alone. He's cross that nothing was discussed, that he couldn't bring himself to mention Jim, that he said, "*I* am having dinner in Los Gatos tonight." His parents will change, he thinks. I doubt it. That is how the world is.

EASTER SUNDAY. Behind Los Gatos, walking through the monastery grounds and up into the hills. The guard monk, the one with the Corona Corona cigars, accosts me with a stupid question about English grammar: "When should you use single inverted commas as opposed to double inverted commas?" He is a bore.

I have never seen it so lush. There is a profusion of weeds and wild flowers: sourgrass, miner's lettuce, dandelion, California poppy in bloom, new leaf on escallonia and poison oak, white feathery pom-poms of blossom on eucalyptus. No pungent scent now of fennel, but smells of greenness, of things growing. A brook in full spate where last October there was a dried-up water-course and silence. San José spread out below us with its dark pines and office-block temples, and there is no smog in this changeable, blustery weather.

A grove of olives: new silvery leaves, and last year's fruit ungathered on the branches or squelched underfoot.

I think of the days spent up here in my sickness—the fall heat, the shafts of sunlight, the dryness and dust—and I realize how attached I've become to this landscape, that it's grown into me as much as a distant view of Dartmoor or Haldon, the slit of the Exe estuary, the cathedral's twin towers.

[79]

I cook dinner for twelve at Katya's. One of those rare parties at which the chemistry between people is superb. Dennis and Paul captain teams for charades; Anne, who isn't aware that the sexual orientation of half the guests is different, tries to mime "King" in *A Connecticut Yankee in King Arthur's Court*. Mystified, we venture "hat", "uniform", and (several times) "queen" (as in Elizabeth). "Why did you keep saying *queen*?" she asks. "I kept pointing at David—King! King!" I glance at Phil, and we both fold up in helpless laughter.

Katya, mischievously, has asked Sarah and Harriet (who are together again) to pop in for a drink; she wants Phil to say "I've heard so much about you!" Neither turns up; another crisis, Katya says, is brewing, or by now has fermented. How many crises do there have to be before the mixture explodes?

XII

LOS ANGELES. Suddenly, after the wettest winter since 1849, the temperature is eighty-five degrees and the sun is with us all day. I drive down with Katya to stay at her cousin's. Irina has been married seven times to four different men, and is depressed because her plans for an eighth marriage—to one of her former husbands—have not materialized. She is a pleasant, relaxed, interesting woman; and I'm happy just to talk to her and Katya and sunbathe in her garden or by the ocean—she lives at Redondo Beach, only minutes from the sea. I tell myself I ought to be exploring gay Los Angeles, but I can't be bothered. Three years ago I trolled up and down the Santa Monica Boulevard, gazing at the "hitch-hikers" and thumbing rides myself. Now I lie on the sand, reading a novel set in sixth-century Byzantium, listen to the sea, and watch the beautiful surfers.

Being near the ocean, Redondo Beach is without smog. Not so inland at the moment; driving up the Pasadena Freeway to the Norton Simon Museum I pass close to downtown LA, and the tops of the skyscrapers are almost invisible. None of the mistiness is fog; it's all petrol fumes. What this must do to the health of the Angelinos, I guess, is something worse than sore throats and streaming eyes.

San Francisco is not old even by American standards, but it gives one the feeling it has lasted, and, earthquakes or not, that it will last. It has that rich blend of setting, architecture, lifestyle and atmosphere which makes any great city different from any other—unique, of itself, a quality that is only San Franciscan, Parisian, Venetian, etcetera. Los Angeles has nothing of this. In area it is the biggest city in the world (ninety miles across) and, together with its satellites and suburbs, it has a population of nine million; but it has only existed in its present huge and sprawling shape since the Second World War. You feel it will not, unlike San Francisco, last, that it will vanish as suddenly as it came into being, choked to death by its exhaust fumes. Not so long ago it must have been an earthly paradise—a thin coastal strip at the foot of the mountains, an almost ideal climate, golden beaches and glorious warm surf. Now it's a spectacular monument to the human capacity for destroying the environment—a ruin achieved not over centuries, but in half an average man's life-time.

"You'll hate it," people said before I first came here. "It's all smog and freeways." All smog and freeways it is, but I don't hate it. I usually enjoy Los Angeles—for a brief while. I'd go mad, however, if I lived here. I don't find its freeways confusing, though they're invariably traffic-packed; at all times of the day it is rush hour. Unlike anywhere else in the world, where a motorway is a relief, it's relaxing here to drive in the stop-go of traffic lights and one-way systems. Angelinos have no concept of car-pool, unlike San Franciscans; in ninety-nine out of a hundred cars there is only one person. The waste of petrol! The cost of petrol! The stink, the smog caused by petrol!

Los Angeles does have its attractions, of course. For a European, to be in Hollywood, or to find oneself standing on Sunset Boulevard, is initially as dream-like, as awesome, as the sight of Buckingham Palace or the Eiffel Tower is to an American. Sunset Boulevard! Can little old me *really* be here? The Hollywood Sign is indubitably impressive and it doesn't look, despite Dory Previn's song, as if it's constantly saying "cheese". The houses and gardens up in the mountains at the back of Hollywood are beautiful. (Those of neurotic Beverley Hills are not.) Cypresses everywhere: parts of LA are great garden suburbs— the buildings almost entirely hidden by trees. I love the eternal sunlight and the heat: the evening heat in summer when the mountains, reddish at this time of day, glow like an enormous hot brick, and seem to gasp with relief that the intense baking has finished for a few hours. The sunsets over the ocean—long bands of vivid orange—and the star-studded skies, nowhere better seen than from the Hollywood Bowl (smog permitting): I remember a concert there, Bartók, Liszt and Brahms, played by the Los Angeles Philharmonic under Giulini; as it began, search-lights were pointed at the sky to tell planes to keep their distance, and every pause in the music was filled with the whispers of a million crickets. The night wind was warm on the skin—we needed no clothes other than shorts. Touch, as well as the ear, satisfied.

And another delight is surfing in a rough sea at Malibu.

THE NORTON SIMON has at least one major painting by anybody of any significance from Botticelli to Picasso—with four curious omissions: no Giotto, Constable, Turner, or Leonardo. The best Sisley I've ever seen—a snowy landscape so cold it draws you in till you feel the ice. More Degas than in the Jeu de Paume; fine collections of Henry Moore sculptures and Picasso drawings of bulls. Rembrandt's *Titus*; Zurbarán's only still life.

The museum is large; after two hours I can absorb no more though I haven't seen everything. It started only thirty years ago; almost all the exhibits, therefore, must have previously been in private hands. In this brief period it has amounted to something that can rival—for example—the Rijksmuseum. And it's the work of one man. The speed of it—is that only possible in Los Angeles, the city that's grown from almost nothing to the world's largest conurbation in forty years? As if the inhabitants know it can't last?

MY ONLY GAY MOMENTS are eating with Scott—an old friend—at a gay restaurant in Pasadena. (The song may revel in the fact that Pasadena is where the grass is greener, but the smog is so bad here that it's killed the palm trees. The city replaced them with plastic palm trees. The smog then rotted the plastic. Or so I'm told; I guess the story is apocryphal—Pasadena has palms like anywhere else. And the little old ladies of both sexes look alive and well.) Scott's house, in Glendale, is in one of LA's leafier corners. An odd house, full of character, tea-planter style on a hill of San Franciscan gradient, surrounded by trees and hanging, trailing flowers. But it stinks of cats, which isn't even preferable to car exhaust.

WE WENT DOWN, and return, on 101; Highway 1, the pretty route, is closed at Malibu, Big Sur, and Pacifica—washed away by the storms this February. But 101 has compensations—the detour over the San Marcos pass is a proper mountain road: the landscape all green, and I remember it withered by months of sun. The coast at Santa Barbara is the California of one's dreams and fantasies: mountains almost tumbling into the golden sands and Riviera-blue sea. Three years ago on Highway 1, I saw Big Sur shrouded in fog, and I came back over the San Bernardino Mountains: soaring peaks, pine woods, great boulders. Distant LA was hidden in a smog cloud, an unnatural purple. The Joshua trees, scrub and sand of the Mojave desert; then groves of almond, peach, nectarine, orange, lemon, and apricot in the Sacramento valley. This time, by 101, from San Luis Obispo to Salinas, a long, long, green plain.

HARRIET IS NOT THRILLED that Sarah disappeared at Easter, for ten days this time. She hints to Katya that the balloon is about to go up. Watch this space!

Gary calls from Spearfish. He doesn't think he can cope with a trip to San Francisco; the big city would unnerve him. It isn't *that* big, I point out. Well . . . he wants to go down to Las Vegas as soon as he graduates, and from there to Dallas at the end of the summer to get settled in. It's a pity we won't meet, he says, but perhaps "it wasn't meant to be." A very flaky individual, this guy; he has a lover in Dallas, I presume, and for some reason doesn't like to tell me. As Americans say, it's time he got his ass in gear.

TWO MURDERS, CARBON COPIES of each other in the evidence, motives and verdicts. A youth, portrayed by the defence as "confused", "from a difficult home background", kills an older gay man, chops the body up with an axe, and burns it and the victim's house, then drives off with his car, money and various possessions. The defence rests on "He made a pass at me." (No witnesses corroborate this statement.) In both trials, the jury is so scandalized by the thought of a man making a pass at another man that they bring in not-guilty verdicts, despite the fact that the murderers *confessed* to their crimes, and one of them had been living in a sexual relationship with the person he killed. The leader of Sonoma County's

[84]

Coalition for Human Rights (not a gay organization) says that this means if he winked at a woman she could now slaughter him with an axe, burn his body, confess, and go free. It wouldn't happen, of course; it's not straights who are denied justice.

Other recent events: an ambulance driver refuses to take a Castro man suffering from peritonitis to hospital because the patient is homosexual . . . Oregon throws out a gay rights bill . . . gays are beaten up and robbed on the 24 Divisadero bus . . .

THE MAYOR OF CASTRO STREET by Randy Shilts is essential reading for anyone who wishes to discover how and why San Francisco became gay Mecca. It's also essential reading for the student of politics, for it is a fascinating account of the struggle for, and the manipulation of, political power: an inefficient, conservative administration, out of touch with the needs of the day, being swept aside by reforming elements that are destroyed by the assassin's bullet.

One may think that the political manoeuvrings of a city council are small beer, but San Francisco's mayor and Board of Supervisors wield far more power than their British equivalents. The mayor is no ceremonial figurehead, but the chief executive; San Francisco's government is the only one in the United States that rules not just the city but the surrounding county too. And small though it is, San Francisco has national prestige and influence quite out of proportion to its size.

The mayor of Castro Street in Shilts's book is Harvey Milk, the first openly gay public official anywhere. He was elected to the Board of Supervisors in 1977, and with the real mayor, George Moscone, was shot dead a year later by Dan White, ex-policeman, ex-supervisor. The book is extremely good on Milk as man and politician, and charts his rise to fame with meticulous detail. It is also excellent on the killings and the subsequent travesty of a trial—Dan White was found not guilty of murder but of voluntary manslaughter; the ineffective prosecution was possibly in cahoots with the defence, and the jury was packed with working-class anti-gay conservatives from Dan White's constituency. Ludicrous evidence purporting to show that the accused was not a cold-blooded murderer was allowed in court: his addiction to cupcakes and junk food, one psychiatrist said, caused his body metabolism to change. The jury believed this. The gay community, on hearing the verdict, reacted with unprecedented anger: they smashed the windows and doors of City Hall, petrol-bombed police cars, and sent over a hundred policemen to hospital. The police retaliated by assaulting gays in Castro and destroying the Elephant Walk.

The historical account of the American gay movement in the 1970s is well done, as is the history of Castro itself—its development from a working-class Irish community, living in tumbledown housing, to the present gay ghetto with its smart, chic Victorians. Why San Francisco, as opposed to anywhere else, became gay Main Street is given full and interesting explanation—it has not been a phenomenon solely of recent years, but has its roots deep in the city's origins and its century-old reputation as the most relaxed, carefree, and colourful of places.

Journalistic hyperbole sometimes mars the writing, and it is a pity that the implied audience is the San Francisco gay—had the author been aware of readers outside Castro, some of the assumptions and details would have been a little less confusing. His obvious dislike of liberal, aloof Dianne Feinstein means that she fills more of the text than is necessary; the ebullient and affable George Moscone, on the other hand, is not given enough space. A serious omission, too, is an analysis of *why* Dan White killed Moscone and Milk. The conspiracy theory is interesting, however—White may have been egged on by policemen who strongly disapproved of Moscone's regime for its pro-gay stance and its determination to clamp down on corruption and violence. There is no doubt that some policemen regard White as a hero for what he did, and have comforted and consoled him during his imprisonment; in 1977 they were discussing the possibility of "removing" Moscone and his liberal police chief, Charles Gain. That the San Francisco police department is still in many ways corrupt and violent is borne out by a recent series of articles in the newspapers, describing the unnecessary beating of suspects—particularly if they are gay or Latino—, the training of recruits in violent methods, and the refusal to take steps against thugs physically assaulting gay people.

Harvey Milk had many premonitions that he would be

murdered. "If a bullet should enter my brain, let that bullet open every closet door," he said in a tape-recorded message found after his death. The bullet that killed him has not opened every closet door, but it has given the gays of San Francisco unprecedented political clout. Their votes subsequently elected Feinstein, and no politician here would now run for office without seeking an endorsement from the gay political clubs. Many openly gay people hold important positions in the city (Feinstein has certainly been aware of her debts), but none has the stature or the charisma of Harvey Milk.

PHIL AND I HAVE ACQUIRED a *huge* dildo. I suppose it could provide some variety to our sex games, but it's the childishness of buying such a thing that I like. It has a cock head at either end. However, I doubt if we'll be using it much!

XIII

THE CORONA CORONA MONK asked Harriet to go out with him. "So she must have something to offer," Katya says, a little enviously.

"She just gives out come-to-bed signals," I answer. "What would you have done if he'd asked *you* for a date?"

"I'd have said no, of course."

"Did she accept the invitation?"

"Sure she did."

They went wining and dining and dancing. Sarah has not been informed—she is still dithering about whether she should leave for good. One day she is, the next she isn't. But, Harriet wants to know from Katya, is the monk crazy? He has told her a long story about not being a monk at all, that he's really employed on secret surveillance work for some intelligence-gathering organization. In *Los Gatos*? I say, incredulous. What on earth is there in rural, upper-middle-class Los Gatos to spy on? Communists, drug-runners, men from Mars? Katya agrees—she told Harriet it was merely a bit of silly boasting. "I think I'm getting paranoid," Harriet says. "It's the loneliness."

You ought to apologize to David for the shabby way you treated him, Katya tells her. Harriet admits she did treat me badly and says she *would* like to apologize.

TO TAHOE. It's good to drive out of the city, and go on driving for hours, even if the Sacramento Valley on a wet cloudy day has little that's interesting to look at. But soon we reach the foothills of the Sierras and there are fir forests and boulders—like Scotland, though on a much grander scale. We climb and climb. The rain turns to sleet. The snow-line! We worry that we didn't bring chains, but decide to press on, though the Donner Pass—which we have to use as all other routes are still closed—is nearly eight thousand feet above sea level. Snow everywhere, dazzling in the brief moments of sun; glimpses of huge summits. Christmas card scenery—trees bent under the snow. Twenty feet deep on the ground in places, I guess.

Lake Tahoe is cold blue, icy green and freezing turquoise; I'm reminded of looking last August from the plane into the Arctic Ocean—the same colours, beautiful and utterly uninviting. Summer chalets in the trees by the lakeshore, not visited by their owners since autumn—snow piled so high on their roofs that they're like pictures from a children's book of fairy stories. Some totally buried; the only sign that a house is there is a gable, a chimney. One has collapsed—a tangled mess of wood and snow. We eat hamburgers and french fries at Stateline, and I change from shorts and tee-shirt to jeans and two sweaters: the temperature is thirty-eight degrees. We cross from California into Nevada, and gamble in a casino.

We're only five hours from the Bay, where it is seventy degrees and never experiences frost. What contrasts California provides! More than anywhere else I've seen. Once, at 10 a.m., the temperature ninety plus, I gazed at the granite and snow of Mount Whitney. Turning round, I was looking at desert—scrub, salt, a dried-up lake: the hinterland of the hottest, driest place on earth—Death Valley.

BEETHOVEN'S FOURTH PIANO CONCERTO, a favourite of my mother's and *her* mother's and mine. It pleases me that it's spoken to three generations; it puts me in touch with the two before me.

WHAT DO I REQUIRE IN A LOVER? That he has a beautiful body to rouse me sexually and which goes on and on rousing me sexually for a long time. That he wants to get fucked. That sex is inventive, uninhibited, frequent, and satisfying. That we part amicably if it doesn't work. Without all that, there is no difference between a lover and a friend.

I like living together, sharing space, though it's not of paramount importance. I like sleeping together, curling round him at night, hearing him breathe. It's good if we both enjoy the gay scene, though similar attitudes to life and temperaments, and

[89]

respect for one another's share of the space, are more important than similar interests. I don't need him for security, or because the world prefers couples. Till-death-do-us-part promises are crap, and so are demands for sexual fidelity, and romanticism of the gazing-into-his-eyes, walking-hand-in-hand-into-the-sunset sort.

I used to think differently, and paid some severe penalties for doing so. I may have lost something in the process, on the road from there to here, but it's not something I regret.

I could change my mind about all this: I could still get swept off my feet, I suppose. But I doubt it. I don't want or need to be swept anywhere.

THE WILD BACK ROOM OF THE JAGUAR, Friday night, 1 a.m. Three years ago at this weekend hour, a couple of hundred men would have been here, kissing and fucking and sucking and poking and prodding and pulling. Now, such is the effect of the AIDS scare, there are perhaps twenty or thirty. Only one man, a good-looking slim black, allows himself to be screwed. If AIDS has stopped fucking with total strangers, it hasn't stopped oral sex. I spend an hour and a half being sucked by a dozen different mouths, always pulling away just before orgasm—I haven't yet found the right guy. I end up with two hunks who are possibly brothers—dark curly hair, hairy bodies; Jewish, I think. One of them has easily the biggest cock of the whole night; I have to suck that. But they're very cautions about contact—no kissing, fucking or sucking me; it's all hands and spit. They like my body as much as I like theirs; that's evident from the caresses. Orgasm, in one of the hands, isn't the greatest—is it ever, this way?

I sucked one cock (not to the point of orgasm) and kissed one man. Enough to give me AIDS? No, unless it's transmitted in saliva. Is it totally stupid to do this from time to time? Perhaps. But . . . do we have to lose the whole life-style of orgies, of tricking, which is such an exhilarating change from sex in a one-to-one relationship? Obviously the Jaguar is not making much money: how long before it has to shut? And the baths? There's a chilling irony here—the freedom we've won in the 1960s and 1970s to have this kind of life is less likely to be taken from us by the law or born-again Christianity than by our own fears of a deadly disease.

Next day, driving past the Jaguar, we see an old grey-haired woman leaning out of the top-floor window, shaking a duster. I'm told she is the owner's mother—the top floor is her flat, self-contained with its own entrance. She presumably knows what goes on downstairs. That men suck cock, fuck . . . and get AIDS. Extraordinary.

THIS MORNING IS NOT THE BEST TIME to write, with work-men digging the street up; the pneumatic drills are so close they could just as well be in our living-room.

Events in Britain seem more interesting than events here: Thatcher's called an election for early June and *Gay News* has ceased to publish. A great many people connected with *Gay News* appear to have suffered financially in the crash, including me. Gay Men's Press, who sold books through *Gay News* mail order, won't now get what they are owed for all those copies of *The Milkman's On His Way* and others. So they can't give me my royalties. Not an enormous sum compared with *Gay News's* debts, but it is my air fare home and half my income tax for this year. I am assured I will get paid; it's all a matter of arranging a bank loan—but the money should have been in *my* bank seven weeks ago.

The role of *Gay News* was more important than that of any other gay newspaper. It dominated the market in Britain as no single gay journal does here; it was literate, intelligent, useful—and necessary. It was often the only link isolated people in the provinces had with the larger gay world. Its book pages were second to none. All this destroyed—because of selfishness and greed.

THE ESTUARY IS NOW IN THE BOOKSHOPS HERE. Reviews in England have been indifferent, and sales are not as good as those of *The Milkman*; but it has, briefly, made the alternative best-seller charts. *Gay News*, in its final issue, carried a piece on it by Rosanna Hibbert, an extremely homophobic lesbian, who laughed at the whole idea of a publishing house catering solely for gay men. I doubt if she'd say the same thing about the

various women's presses. And yesterday I said the book pages of
Gay News were second to none!

SUMMER STARTED ON MAY 6. The day before, the rain was
torrential—but that was the end of it. A fortnight after, record
high temperatures in San Francisco. Ninety plus in our back
yard; evenings, walking about Castro in shorts. But, here in the
city, it doesn't last. The Sacramento valley has heated up now
and is pulling in cool air from the ocean. Which means, for us,
fog night and morning, no sun till noon, and a cold wind when
the fog burns off. Yet in the South Bay there is perpetual sun
from dawn till dusk and no wind. I'm driving down to Los
Gatos three times a week to write in Katya's garden and soak up
the sun; already I'm mahogany colour.

Katya has a room to let. Phil and I have decided to take it;
when I return to England he'll stay on there till Christmas. At
Katya's we'll have more space, the garden, the peace and quiet,
the mountains; and it's cheaper than this apartment. And sun—
as I write this in San Francisco, it's afternoon and still foggy.

But the fog can be a beautiful, spectacular phenomenon.
Yesterday, driving up the Junipero Serra in the gilded evening
light, the fog banks swirled in over the mountains: densely
packed white cotton wool that tumbled, frothed, eddied. San
Francisco was obliterated, suffocated in that cocoon. At a distance it could have been snow-capped sierras glittering in the
sun.

AT LAST WE FIND A DISCO where we can dance, where the
music is good—the Stud, a ramshackle bar on ramshackle
Folsom, a "young crowd" scene totally different from the rest
of Folsom's leather and clone watering-holes. Wednesday is
Golden Oldies night. So we wanted to hold your hand, twisted
like we did last summer, had Saturday night fever, laid all your
love on me, and, so brief is pop life that it's already an oldie, did
anything Hall and Oates wanted us to do. We shall certainly do
it again.

DRINKING GIN AT A QUARTER TO FIVE in the afternoon when
the earthquake destroys Coalinga. In the garden at Los Gatos

we feel nothing; had I been just down the road in San José the story would be different. Avril was working in the office we share at the university: her desk skidded across the room; our books fell off the shelves; our papers scattered like feathers. Outside, the ground heaved. She ran out of the building, as did everyone else. But no damage, no injuries.

It must have been very severe—San José is a hundred and fifty miles from the epicentre.

I read that there is a ten per cent chance of a major earthquake—eight on the Richter scale—in San Francisco *soon*. But a forty per cent chance of it occurring in Los Angeles. LA would be wiped off the map: the shortest-lived big city in history.

THE PHONE RINGS. Harriet! She apologizes at length for the way she has treated me. So many problems this year with Sarah; she really was too disturbed and upset to know what she was doing. If I'm ever in Los Gatos, I must call in for a drink and a chat. I say, guardedly, that I know it isn't easy to apologize, and thank her for doing so. The conversation drifts on to how we coped with work this semester . . .

There is method in her madness, Katya and I agree. I'm a transient; Katya is not. To restore her relationship with Katya it's necessary to mend fences with me—and she needs to restore that relationship. If Sarah goes—and she has said that, though she hasn't yet planned out her summer, she is going to spend her time as far away from Los Gatos as possible—Harriet will be quite alone. (What, I wonder, has happened to the monk?)

Katya wants to regain access to Harriet's pool. Soon after I tell her of the phone call, she's gone up there to swim!

MY BIRTHDAY, and it's the hottest day of the year so far. So it was on my eighth birthday when all the tulip petals withered in the heat and dropped on to the fallen cherry blossom, streaks of blood on the white grass. To Katya's, where plans for the evening are curiously vague.

"We are to have a drink with Sarah and Harriet," she tells me. "So they can meet Phil."

"I don't really want to do that," I say. "I don't imagine for one second that *he* does, either. And what about food?"

"Oh, we'll have something to nibble somewhere."

I suspect she and Phil are taking me out to a restaurant.

Last week I found lying around in the apartment an envelope addressed to Phil, with Katya's name on it as the sender. He refused to tell me what was in it, but when I pressed him he said he'd written to her for advice—he was worried about our relationship. I felt embarrassed by this confession, and mildly annoyed.

Katya insists that we have a couple of drinks in downtown Los Gatos, which is odd as her kitchen is, as usual, overflowing with every variety of booze; after that, to Harriet's. Hadn't we better wait for Phil to arrive from work? I ask. But she says Anne will bring him up. Harriet and Sarah are all smiles, all welcomes—and they give me a birthday present! A bottle of Dutch gin. We've hardly downed our first cocktail when Katya drags me off to *her* house. So much for mending fences.

The driveway is full of cars. What is going on? I ask, but have not long to wait for an answer. Indoors are Phil, Tim, Anne, Dennis and Paul, Avril, Alan and Nils, Kevin, Lee, Julian, Robert and Matt, Janos and Jim, Maureen; a great pile of cards and presents, a turkey dinner on the table, and everyone singing "Happy Birthday To You!" Phil has stage-managed this; Katya was the decoy to whisk me elsewhere while the guests and the dinner arrived, and her letter to Phil was copies of a map to tell people who had never been to her house how to find it. He was clever enough to invent a lie that, more than any other, would divert my attention from the *real* contents of the envelope!

I've been involved two or three times before in planning such parties, but I've never been on the receiving end. I'm embarrassed, giggly, sure I'm incapable of rising to the occasion . . . but what a sweet, gorgeous thing to do! Why should anyone care, I say to myself over and over again—and worry that I'm not being properly appreciative. Overwhelmed, I suppose, is the one word that sums up my feelings.

It's an immense pleasure to see how well these friends from different bits of my life get on together, gay and straight, work colleagues, San Francisco, Los Gatos, San José. Particularly good to see Alan, who has travelled fifty-five miles despite phlebitis, diabetes and emphysema.

[94]

We eat, drink, talk, and dance in the garden this marvellous, hot, enchanted May evening till long past midnight and watch a huge moon, white as bone, hang above the Santa Clara Mountains . . .

XIV

SEXUAL PROMISCUITY THIS WEEKEND. Phil and I at the Watergarden; he's picked up by a man with, he tells me afterwards, "a washboard stomach". For me, a Frenchman who, when we've screwed, wants a date, my address and phone number, wants to begin an affair *tout de suite*. More pleasurable are a couple of teenage Canadians on holiday here, a slim blond and his friend, a muscular guy with dark curly hair. Firm youthful buns . . .

Phil and I spend Sunday having sex, discussing sex, analysing last night's sex, saying we talk and think far too much about sex. I exude sexuality, he says, a lazy male arrogant sexuality that constantly turns him on. But, he tells me, I'm too obsessed with sex, and I admit he's right—it's the result of living in Sin City.

Overshadowing this hedonistic paradise is AIDS. The newspapers and the TV are, if not reaching saturation point, certainly giving the subject enormous coverage at the moment: because it now affects heterosexuals. I'm not in the bathhouses every night. Once a month, perhaps, on average. When I've fucked people other than Phil I've rarely "ingested body fluids" as the precautionary literature puts it. But what substances pass through the skin of my cock, the lining of my mouth? The long incubation period, up to two years—how many men have I had in that time? The only real precaution is to screw with one regular partner. I don't think I'm a high risk, but I have obviously been in situations where there has been *some* risk. What sexually active gay man in the past two years has not?

There are questions, but no answers. Are we all going to die? It seems so improbable—and in that is the core of the problem: the it-only-happens-to-the-other-person syndrome, as in plane crashes and wrecked cars, means AIDS will spread.

THE LAST PROGRAMME of the ballet season. Béjart's *Firebird* is a disappointment, but Christiansen's *Il Distratto* is as hilarious a send-up of every dance stereotype as is the Royal Ballet's *Élite Syncopations*. *Beach Blanket Babylon*, a revue at a downtown San Francisco theatre club, is a more satisfying evening, despite the heat and the crowded smoky room. SF is particularly good on pub and club theatre, intimate sophisticated revue. This one tells the story of how Snow White left the Bay to seek her fortune in New York, but sensibly chose in the end to return here. It is a celebration of the chauvinism of this most chauvinist of places, a good example of the old adage that a San Franciscan would prefer to starve in a gutter of his own city than live in a penthouse elsewhere.

It's slick, amusing, and extremely well done. Multitudinous costume changes and the most bizarre hats. I'm as caught up as any native in the mood of it. Native? I now have an entry in the local telephone directory. I, too, belong!

A WEEKEND AT CLEAR LAKE, at a gay motel next to a gay bar in a village of only thirty houses—something impossible to imagine anywhere else than in California. Clear Lake is in the mountains, three hours by car north of San Francisco. We drive over the Calistoga Pass: fresh green May leaves on all the trees. It's not high enough for snow. It's hot: I sunbathe nude by the motel's open-air jacuzzi, and the little white strip normally covered gets burned and blistered. Meals out; walking in the mountains; young bird life on the lake: ducks with cortèges of ducklings, fluffy yellow toys. The bar is run by a pleasant Scots–Yugoslav and his Mexican–Filippino lover; on the Saturday they throw a party to which we're invited, and all the rural gays from the remote mountain fastnesses arrive, looking for someone to spend the night with. So, suddenly the motel is full of just-met couples, and our sleep is punctuated with groans and pants through the paper-thin walls.

We talk incessantly about our relationship—I have to return to England in September; is that the end? What commitment on my side, on his side? The discussion ranges from warm, amiable companionship to heated arguments. (The latter when we've been drinking.) I can't articulate my thoughts properly until the journey home. Yes, Phil might be the man I want to spend the rest of my days with. I don't know. I'd need not months, but a year, two years, more perhaps, to say to myself: this is so obviously true and so obviously important I'd give up everything to share my life with him permanently in California.

Then he produces his bombshell. He's decided not to come to Los Gatos at the end of June, but to stay in San Francisco. Katya's house is inconveniently far from his work, and . . . if we're living apart, he'll feel the pain of the six thousand miles of our separation in September less acutely. He'll return to his room at Robert and Matt's (still empty) and force himself into some kind of independence from me. I produce every argument I can think of to dissuade him, but he's adamant. We'll see each other at weekends, he repeats over and over, just as we did last fall. Wasn't that the best time? We'll go to Reno for the gay rodeo, in August.

I feel bewildered and hurt, then tell myself: David, it's what you deserve. It's entirely your own fault. What have you chucked away?

He's crying, silently, and I pull off the road. In a green damp field we make love with such thoughtful sweetness I can't recall anything so tender.

"I love you, I love you," I say. "I love you!" And mean it more than I've ever said those words to anyone.

MID-AFTERNOON, walking down Collingwood, I glance at a window and see the blond to whom I sometimes wave, reading a book I guess, though all that's visible is his head and shoulders. He looks up; I walk on, glance back—he's still looking, so I slow down, stop. A long mutual stare. He stands; he's wearing nothing but shorts, and he's drinking a glass of white wine. He beckons to me. I go up the steps to the house. A minute later we've ripped off our clothes and are in bed. A first-class fuck.

The utter casualness of this encounter excites me much more than the hunt—so deliberate—at the baths.

He phones, and we agree to meet. Another Yugoslav. "I want to play some rather more sophisticated games next time," he says.

HOW DO I RECONCILE that experience with the damp green field on the way home from Clear Lake? I can't. Do I have to? I don't know.

SEATTLE. I spent a long weekend here in September 1980, staying with an old friend, Hugh, and his wife, Ellen. I was stung by a fierce North American bee. My antibodies can cope with a British bee, but not the Washington State variety: my left foot was so swollen I couldn't wear a shoe, nor a slipper, and finally not even a sock. Descending from the Greyhound bus in San Francisco at 7.30 in the morning, I limped home, one foot bare, the other shod; Sin City's commuters, reconciled to almost anything one imagines, gave me a wide berth. I was virtually unable to walk for a week.

Nothing so unpleasant this time; just clouds which obscure the Olympic and the Cascade Mountains, and the coldest June temperatures I've ever experienced. In 1980 Mount Rainier seemed to float, pink, white and serene, and the jagged Olympics were black against the evening sun. All this from Hugh's bathroom which has some of the finest panoramas in Seattle, a city almost as fine for its views as San Francisco. For it, too, has hills, albeit less dramatic, and water—the vast calm of the Puget Sound—and white clean architecture, and the Space Needle, which rivals our Trans-Am Pyramid as a remarkable essay in how concrete can become eye-catching fantasy. The Space Needle, like the Pyramid, is the city's most well-known distinguishing mark. It looks a bit like London's Telecom Tower, with lifts and a revolving restaurant; but it's much more appealing. The background to Seattle's bold white architecture in summer is not Californian burnt grass and ochre earth, but greenness—fir forests, fields and moorland that are as familiar with drizzle as is a Scottish brae. After San Francisco and Los Angeles it seems peculiar to find a modern American city in a landscape like this, as if Seattle were where the Kyle of Lochalsh usually is.

Hugh and I follow old interests—we eat Japanese, get drunk, listen to opera, and he smuggles me into the Press box of the Kingdome, the luxurious stadium of the Seattle Sounders, whom we see beaten by Fiorentina of Italy. Some very good-looking footballers on the pitch. Hugh teaches at Washington State University; Ellen says he is acutely depressed. His work no longer satisfies: he believes he's an old fart. I'm afraid my visit will not help; my "success" (I wouldn't call it that, but he may do so) is not likely to improve things. However, she says I've cheered him immensely. Soon they are going to Europe, for a year, renting a decrepit palazzo in Venice. Which, she hopes, will give him the impetus he needs.

Gay Seattle. Kinnear Park I nose out by chance—not empty even in mid-afternoon despite the wild, wooded, almost inaccessible cliff where only the sex drive would drive men; old ladies and their dogs stay on the more level ground below and above. The Continental Baths has the biggest jacuzzi I've ever bubbled in, positively Roman in size. AIDS has not become the scare it is in San Francisco; this is like old times—busy! For me, its most exciting feature is its gloryholes, and I spend hours having my cock sucked by anonymous Seattle mouths. But eventually come with a curly-haired blond on a bed, a macho footballer with girl-friends. "I don't often use this place," he says. I hope he's enjoying it enough with me to think of the pleasures he could have if he'd emerge from the closet. Who's he trying to kid? I'm not the first man whose load has shot in *his* throat.

I CAME TO SEATTLE in 1980 from Vancouver, in a car with three young lady librarians; we had all been at a book conference. Vancouver I did not find the beautiful city everybody said it was, apart from the refurbished nineteenth-century quarter, Gastown; but the splendid backcloth of mountain and evergreen forest can be observed from most of the dull urban streets. I bought a cast-iron frying pan here which I lugged home to England, and a necklace with a jade killer-whale pendant. I stumbled, again by chance, on the gay beach, and had sex—but with whom and how I can't remember. I do remember a trip to Vancouver Island: a long, long journey by coach and boat. Narrow inlets like Norwegian fjords. Victoria, the capital, I was told was so English, but it isn't—a pleasant enough city, however. The Bouchart Gardens, a rich old woman's folly left to please thousands of tourists with almost every variety of flower one can think of. The sense of remoteness—nine tenths of this island is not only uninhabited, it's virtually unexplored. I have a very distant relative by marriage, Ada, who lives in a cabin in the forests, far from roads, supermarkets, TV, all aspects of twentieth-century civilization. Why, how is she here?

ON THE FLIGHT FROM SEATTLE to a San Francisco of eighty-one degrees I see Mount Rainier, an extinct volcano gleaming with snow, majestic and aloof: and all the other summits—Mount Hood, Mount Jefferson, Mount Adams, Mount Shasta. And Mount St Helens, grey ash, its top blown to the stratosphere, the whole landscape to the east devastated. It exploded on my birthday three years ago. When I flew above it two months later it was still very happily puffing, and spewing out vast quantities of debris. Ruining the world's weather. It's difficult today to believe that: a picture postcard sunset, Clear Lake and Great Crater Lake (which must have been a *huge* volcano) beneath us in absolute clarity. As we descend to SF International I can see everything in minute detail—the fog swirling into the San Andreas, the light on the water, cars on the bridges, our house on Douglass. It all looks not far short of paradise: I'm glad to be home.

JANOS'S FATHER WRITES "I love you, son—but I can't accept that a man who takes another man to bed is choosing to do something natural and normal." *Choosing*? He's very welcome to go home whenever he wants, but he mustn't bring any of his "friends". A case, I think, of love meaning "I'll love you when you're more like me."
Janos is hurt and angry.

SOME ILL-INFORMED DIMWITS in the San Francisco police department have written to Mayor Feinstein suggesting that the Democrat Convention (scheduled here for the summer of 1984) should be held in another city, in case the delegates catch AIDS. The mayor is furious. But the leader of the North Carolina delegation (also a woman) says *all* the North Carolinans are coming, whatever.
"California, we hear, is Nutsville," she says. "Life in the

Carolinas is so boring that we're going to San Francisco to get some of the action. Be damned to the consequences!"

The epidemic has reached a new stage—public hysteria. The TV and the Press are, in part, responsible for this—their reports are often sensational or misleading. A TV programme the other night left a suggestion in viewers' minds that AIDS could be caught by casual contact—bumping into a sweaty body on a disco floor. The chief AIDS specialist from San Francisco General Hospital, however, emphasized this week, on the front page of the *Chronicle*, that it was a very difficult disease to catch. An exchange of body fluids—semen passing through minute cracks of the anus or the wall of the rectum into the blood-stream—is an essential prerequisite. *Not* sweat or saliva. There is no evidence that kissing has ever given anyone AIDS (and therefore, I assume, having your cock sucked is harmless). Many live-in long-term lovers of AIDS victims do not have the disease.

But some of the victims have been thrown out by their lovers, been banned from appearing on TV (the camera crew might get it!), turned off buses. And looming over it all is the straight backlash—this terrible condition has been spread by *homosexuals*. That the annual gay parade should be prohibited and the bath-houses closed are two of the milder reactions. Nurses in San José have resigned rather than come near the city's one AIDS patient currently in hospital. Some people even believe it can be caught from doorknobs and toilet seats, and the police department (always San Francisco's most unintelligent authority) has distributed masks for its men to use when handling suspects who may have AIDS.

It's not easy to avoid the general fear—you imagine every new spot or pimple could be Kaposi's sarcoma, when it's obviously acne or an insect bite. Sometimes, as I look down at Castro from 22nd or Liberty, I say to myself "That's Aidsville"—or wonder, in a crowded bar or disco, how many men there have the disease and don't yet know it. I think of London just before the Plague struck in 1665 and ask myself if San Francisco is on the edge of a calamity of similar proportions.

Then try to get it all into some kind of perspective. There's a *much* greater risk of being killed in a car crash or dying of lung cancer.

XV

THE *LONDON SYMPHONY* of Vaughan Williams. It's so long since I heard it that it's like listening to an absolutely new piece. Even in this early attempt the musical language he forged for himself and used with little variation for the rest of his life is there, and obvious—the clusters of pentatonic chords, the uneasy shifts from major to minor in the same key, the ability to disintegrate what he has built up by galloping, runaway rhythmic chaos. The trouble is that there are several Vaughan Williamses—the folksy Englishman; the rhapsodic dreamer; the gruff angry commentator. When all the different personae appear in the same work the result is unsatisfactory, as in this symphony: it is a stylistic mess. The most interesting Vaughan Williams is, with the exception of the *Tallis Fantasia* and the *Pastoral Symphony*, the gruff angry commentator. The fourth and sixth symphonies are his great achievements, rare examples in the twentieth century of symphonic music that has a strong non-musical point. I don't mean they have, in the conventional sense of the word, a programme, but they do seem to be reactions to the political events of the time—the rise of Fascism, the Second World War. Indeed, nearly all Vaughan Williams's music is "about" something: evident in the symphonies that have titles—the *Sea*, the *Pastoral*, the *London*, the *Antartica*—but those that are untitled have a cause, or response, or meaning, too.

The fourth symphony I think one of the half-dozen real masterpieces of the period. It is one long cry of agony, without let-up, an implacable, pitiless marshalling of forces; a musical *Guernica*. I don't know anything quite like it—nothing in Stravinsky, Bartók or Shostakovich comes near to matching its explosive, destructive power. The pitilessness recurs in the one excellent movement of the *Antartica*—where Scott reaches the glacier. Destruction and chaos are also there in *Job*; the great moment is the "Dance of Job's Comforters". Both passages make brilliant and unexpected use of gongs and an organ. Curious that he should have been so good at depicting the negative—and mostly unmemorable with the positive emotions.

RANDOM THOUGHTS. Gay Men's Press still haven't paid, and though I'm not in any immediate financial difficulty, I soon will be.

People who've read *The Estuary* tell me they like it. Janos, only half-way through the book, calls to say how much he's enjoying it, that he thinks it's my best novel so far. One needs kindness like that.

Writing every day, at Katya's or here in the city, a new novel—*Out of the Winter Gardens*. It seems to follow laws of its own, for nothing I plan in my head gets down on paper. The work, as usual, is done in the actual writing. My hero, at the moment, is too old for his years; in chapter one he's not old enough; the dialogue is OK but there's too much of it; and the whole thing is full of flaws and inconsistencies. But I shall enjoy the effort, later on, to pull it together.

Katya's daughter Varvara is in the pokey for picketing a nuclear power station. Katya writes angrily to the *Chronicle*—and the letter is printed.

Phil is sick, on and off, for three weeks—a viral infection of the bowel and inflammation of the prostate. Not an easy patient, but I know well the depression that's caused by being ill, and sympathize. When he recovers we sunbathe for hours on the nude beach at Land's End, and in the evening dance at the I-Beam.

Dinner with Dennis and Paul. Brunch at Tim's. Bridge with Dennis, Alan and Nils. A party with friends at Woodside: a Hockney swimming-pool scene, the California of one's fantasies—heat, sun, wine, beautiful bodies, laid-back talk.

Not a word from Spearfish. I'll pre-empt this situation, soon.

It hasn't rained for seven weeks. In the city, fog night and morning, and a strong afternoon wind that chills the sunlight.

[104]

SARAH HAS GONE. To a room in Peter's house. Harriet, distraught and thrown completely off balance by this, has decided not to spend the summer in Greece; she was to be co-leader of some tourist group, but says she can't now cope with the work involved. Maybe by staying nearby she expects to lure Sarah back.

I MEET A TALL, LANKY BLOND one mid-day on Castro and induce him into my bed. He's from Santa Barbara, a student aged twenty-one, German in origin—blue eyes, a fit, suntanned body. He tells me his life story, and I think, as I so often do when I listen to young gays talking, that growing up now can be very different from when I was a kid—if courage and belief in oneself come early. His lover lived with him for a year in his parents' house when he was nineteen, and the parents were happy with this. Before that, he nearly got married (and loved sex with the girl, though, he adds, he wouldn't now): he's screwed around a great deal since he broke up with the lover, in America and Europe, and immensely enjoyed himself.

No point in regretting that I didn't, or couldn't, live like that in my teens. I've made up for it since.

THE LAST SUNDAY OF JUNE—the Gay Parade, the biggest gay parade in the world, the biggest annual gathering of any kind in San Francisco. The police and the Press report that numbers are down this year because of the AIDS scare, only two hundred thousand people. Three hundred and fifty thousand, the organizers say; the truth, as usual, is probably somewhere in between. Market is closed to traffic—the parade processes along the whole length of it. The pavements on either side are packed with bystanders twelve deep, and many more are watching from the windows above, or clinging to lamp-posts and sitting on the tops of temporarily redundant traffic lights. Strangers talking, laughing with each other; beer is being consumed in great quantities. Pungent smells of marijuana. The weather is beautiful—warm and cloudless.

It's a triumph of organization. It takes four hours to go by, and hundreds of groups are represented: the gay political clubs, Gay Fathers (with their children), Gay Mothers (with *their* children), a cable car full of Parents of Gays, Gay Farmers, Gay Businessmen, Gay Teachers, the Gay Men's Chorus, the Gay Freedom Day Marching Band and Twirling Corps, Gay Karate, Gay Methodists, Gay Catholics (dozens of them), Gay Mormons (five), Gay Atheists (their banners read: CURB YOUR DOGMA— BORN-AGAIN ATHEIST), Gay People in the Arts, Fat Gays, Gay Doctors, gay anything. There are cable cars, vintage cars, ordinary cars, floats, people on foot, motorbikes. The Dykes on Bikes lead, as always, in "a symphony of tuxedos, tee-shirts and black leather" as the *Chronicle* lyrically says. And it's an accurate description—scores of bikes, two girls on each, blasting horns, cheering, shouting, waving. Then the sombre part: the AIDS victims, some in shrouds in a cable car, but most on foot, waving and smiling as much as the dykes. Political heavyweights—our Congresswoman, state senators, the mayor of Berkeley, the gay sheriff of Hayward, the city's supervisors— wanting our votes, but also they're enjoying themselves just being here. Some exquisite drag. We walk behind the last float to City Hall where the thousands mill about on the grass of the Tenderloin, to the puzzlement of the tramps whose open-air home this is. Bands sing and play music here, and speakers speak all afternoon. In nearby streets are rows of portajohns with lengthy queues; the nearest parking lot is quicker, and so many cocks piss through its wire fence into somebody's yard that the trees may wither. Beyond the loos are the hot dog stalls, beer stalls, the innumerable stalls of various groups hawking their own particular version of gay liberation. For two dollars I stand behind a cardboard nun, don a wimple, and have myself photographed with arms round Sister Freeda Peoples and Sister Missionary Position. The crowd is happy, relaxed, enjoying itself; Phil and I talk and joke and flirt with innumerable strangers. My WANNA FUCK? tee-shirt helps: "Had *any* offers?" or "When?" or "No thanks" or "How much?" or even "Yes please" are some of the responses.

Eventually we sit on the grass, drink more beer, and listen to the music. A cute young guy leaps on to an obelisk and begins to harangue the crowd: he's a born-again Christian telling us AIDS is God's curse for screwing with our own sex. The crowd jeer and shout so much his words are lost. Some climb on to the obelisk and snatch the leaflets he's holding, scattering them to the four winds. A girl takes off her clothes and wiggles her bare breasts a few inches from him, then a parade marshal forces him to stop: but a few moments later he's at it again, standing this time on a park bench. Emboldened, I suppose, by the alcohol, I walk up to him and fondle his cock. A closet case! He does not flinch *at all*!! The marshal tells me, in no uncertain tones, to behave myself, and informs the Christian that the police have been asked to remove him. The Christian vanishes, disconsolate, into the crowd, after picking up the few leaflets he can find. I feel sorry for him. In a way, admire him. Oh yes, he's insulting us and deserves what he gets, but there's something pathetic and sad—and brave—about being the odd one out in a quarter of a million happy people. Did he see himself as one of the angels abused in the streets of Sodom, and gain comfort and strength from that thought? But he certainly did not mind my hand stroking his cock. In a year or two will he be marching with the Gay Atheists?

We eat in an unusually deserted Castro (they're all still outside City Hall), then go to La Galleria for a special Gay Freedom Day dance. La Galleria is a converted warehouse miles off on the waterfront side of the Bayshore Freeway. The floor is vast, and though a great crowd is discoing, there is more room to move than at the End-up or the I-Beam. The music is good. Stairs lead to balconies where people look down and watch the dancers; we climb right up to the top and see couples lying about on plush carpets, screwing.

We don't stay long. Friday we were packing, Saturday moving house, today—this. We're exhausted. Monday, I ache in every muscle.

I AM AT KATYA'S NOW, settling in again. Silence. Sun all day. A racoon walking down the middle of the sleepy, dusty road. My room has two windows: outside one is a bottle-brush in full flower and a giant fuschia; outside the other a tangerine tree covered in fruit. The darkness at night is total. Yapping of distant dogs.

I work on the new novel, and in the evenings stay indoors. Watch movies on video. Drink wine. Go daily to the gym.

[107]

Spend little money, and sleep well, though Phil is not in my bed now.

I miss him, of course.

JULY THE FOURTH, AND TO CELEBRATE the loss of the American colonies we are at Alan and Nils's house eating and drinking with almost everyone gay we know and a hundred others. The garden is like a garden restaurant, with tables, waiters, flags and balloons. I flirt with a black who has great biceps and what is obviously a cock of immense proportions.

Sultry weather—ninety, ninety-five. In the evening, at Los Gatos, we watch from the windows fireworks explode downtown. Airless and humid indoors, sweaty in bed, and I fear I won't sleep. Phil is with me tonight. We fuck, and I do sleep. The next day, a delicious cool breeze.

AT A DISCO IN SANTA CLARA I meet a man who really turns me on: loose-limbed and long-legged, very muscly, and a forest of thick dark hair from the throat down. The July the fourth black produced the same desire in me—to be screwed into the middle of next week.

Odd.

I make a date with this guy—and he doesn't turn up.

TERRORIZED NURSES FLEE FROM DEADLY GAY PLAGUE yells a headline in the *Weekly World News*, and what follows is a piece of journalism of the most utterly irresponsible sort. It is intemperate in language—"The wildfire epidemic of lethal AIDS disease has spread a blanket of terror across America so overwhelming that even nurses are quitting their hospital jobs rather than look after its helpless victims"—and untruthful in content—"There are a great many doctors who believe it can be spread through the air or food. It's no longer called the 'gay disease'. Everybody is now in danger of getting it." Doctors have said over and over again that it *cannot* be spread through the air or food, that everybody is *not* in danger of getting it, and that no nurse or physician attending an AIDS patient has ever caught it. The English of this piece one would consider laughable (its splendid mixed metaphor—wildfire spreading an overwhelming blanket) if it were not for the fact that its purpose is to create fear, panic, and an anti-gay backlash.

Recent AIDS news is mildly encouraging: in the past six months there has been a drop in the number of new cases when a doubling of the numbers had been expected. The reasons for this are not known, but speculation revolves round the possibility that a virus is perhaps not the culprit after all; or, if it is, it has mutated, as some flu viruses do, into a benign form. People may have contracted the disease but not so severely that they are prone to opportunistic infections, or they are somehow building up antibodies that can deal with it.

The bath-houses, however, have fallen on really bad times. One in San Francisco went bust recently, and held a bankruptcy sale. What of, I wonder. Gloryholes, empty popper bottles? Men?

XVI

I TAKE OFF, ALONE, FOR A WEEK. Driving south in a seventeen-year-old Corvair which is much admired by every gas station attendant I talk to. Ralph Nader had the Corvair branded as dangerous, so it was withdrawn from the market and now has a rarity value. I can't find anything particularly dangerous about it. This is Nils's car: borrow it, he said; we use the Cadillac (the Fleetwood Brougham d'Élégance!)—drive to the Grand Canyon if you like. The generosity: would any British person do likewise with his car? Old though it is, it has only twelve thousand miles on the clock, and it is in superb condition.

On Aptos Beach I watch dozens of brown pelicans who have made their home on a battered hulk a few yards from the shore. They take to the air in twos and threes and skim low over the water. Their movements are astonishingly graceful—wings outspread, they look like exotic umbrellas floating without effort on the wind currents. But their eyes stare downwards all the time; they float with a purpose. They stab the waves at a very oblique angle—four degrees, maybe five—then zoom, for a moment, just under the surface, reappear and fly on, no doubt having fed well. Arrogant; kings of the sea. The fish population must suffer from massive, constant nervous breakdowns.

The hulk on which the pelicans live was once a dance hall, but it caught on fire in the 1920s and nobody bothered to rebuild it. Once a Mecca for charlestoning humans: noise, smoke-filled air. Now only birds.

MONTEREY, PICTURESQUE in that sense of the word used of fishing ports in Devon and Cornwall: boats, harbour walls. The sea blue-black like Stephens ink, the same colour as the Aegean, Homer's wine-dark. Cliffs, inlets, shell-white sand. Steinbeck's

Cannery Row, but instead of the tarted-up scene I'd imagined—old warehouses converted to Steinbeck souvenir shops—it's dilapidated and largely torn down. I drive round the Monterey Peninsula, famous for its pines, the last bastion on earth of the Monterey cypress; then, on a beach, sunbathe for an hour. Otters lying still as logs in the sea-tangle, or diving, frisking, swimming backstroke. Sea lions toiling slowly up the rocks. Their movements are clumsy, involve a great deal of effort. Not surprising, as they have no arms. Sociable animals. They sit on the rocks, nuzzling and preening, barking their heads off.

Spectacular mountain and cliff road south, to Big Sur. Point Sur is California's Mont St Michel, but instead of an abbey there's a lighthouse; no cluster of huddled buildings, but grass; and the causeway is sand, not road. This is far from anywhere else: not out in the wilds, but beyond the wilds. In the evening I eat salmon in Monterey, at a restaurant overlooking the harbour. Another dazzling performance of otter antics.

A day of sun and sky, rocks, light on a ruffled, wrinkled, heaving sea.

MORE ANIMALS. SEALS ASLEEP, an occasional flipper twitching. Do they dream? Shapeless things. A skunk. The first I've ever noticed; smaller than I'd thought. It is lifting its tail to fill the night air with its evil smell: I do not stop.

But I do stop in Yosemite when I see a fox trotting peacefully up the other side of the road. Very much like an Alsatian, but smaller; dingy and grey in colour. Nasty yellow eyes. Instead of running off as I expect, it halts, turns and looks at me, then opens its slobbery jaws. This I realize is no fox. It's a *wolf*!

It seems to be wondering how I would taste, so I drive on. A moment later its friend comes out of the forest; looks left, looks right, looks left again as a well-trained dog reacts on a pedestrian crossing; then it lollops over the road and disappears between the trees.

THE MONTEREY CYPRESS SURVIVES in crevices in the cliffs, allowing the winter storms to batter it into twisted, violent, writhing shapes. Its foliage is an extraordinarily vivid green, as emerald as fields in Ireland after rain. The sequoias in Yosemite are just as odd—the world's tallest living things, three hundred feet or more in height. (California boasts a crop of ultimates: excluding Alaska, Mount Whitney is the highest mountain in the United States; Bad Water in Death Valley, well below sea level, is the lowest point on the North American continent, and Tahoe the biggest lake; the bristlecone pine is the world's oldest living thing; the Bay Bridge is the longest bridge in the West; etcetera.) The sequoias can't be much younger than the bristlecones: one, called the Grizzly Giant, is two thousand seven hundred years old. The colossal soaring trunks of these trees are reddish in colour, are ramrod straight, and they seem to disappear into the heavens. It's impossible for the eye to absorb all the details. A few have been vandalized—the middle of the trunk of the sequoia known as the California Tree has been cut out. You can walk through it, even drive a car through it.

Why have they endured? They are immune to disease, and they're fire-proof. Yes, fire-proof wood! They have one failing: their roots spread rather than dig deep, so in the winter gales some of them fall over.

YOSEMITE, OF COURSE, IS MAGNIFICENT; particularly the sunken glaciated valley in the heart of the sierras. That glacier worked like a laser beam; the valley walls are three thousand feet of sheer drop. Half Dome is precisely what its name says, a mountain one side of which is vertical, the other a gently sloping curve. At dawn, at sunset, the granite of Half Dome, El Capitan and the Cathedral blushes pink or glows like orange fire. Waterfalls tumble over the edges—Yosemite Falls, though it's the world's second highest waterfall, is not one great single plunge as is Niagara; it hurtles down its mountain-side in three stages. This year, because of the long bad winter, there is a prodigious quantity of snow on the peaks, and the waterfalls are tremendous torrents. In 1980 there was no snow here in July, and I climbed the boulders to the foot of the Bridalveil Falls; now spray soaks me to the skin before I can get near them. The Merced River is icy green and swift—recently melted snow.

I drive to the top of Glacier Point, and gaze down the three thousand feet of wall to the green river, the toy village, the postage-stamp swimming pool, the ant-like cars. Then look up at jagged summits, snow and sky.

At night this sky is thick with stars, and there are shooting stars whizzing across the heavens at unimaginable speeds.

The problem with Yosemite is people. It's famous, accessible, and organized. You cannot, in the valley, get away from the other humans, their litter, their artefacts. But the valley is only one small bit of the National Park, and had I time and inclination I could back-pack and live rough in these mountains for days on end, and see not humans but bears and wolves.

I drive out of the park via Tuolumne Meadows, the unpopular route because nothing lies to the east of the sierras in the way of cities, just the Nevada Desert. Also the road, though an easy climb as far as the ten thousand feet summit of the Tioga Pass, is not easy thereafter. The Tioga was shut this year till the beginning of July; as I drive on, the snow is still deep under the fir trees, and the air is cool. I don sunglasses to stop not sun-dazzle, but snow-glare. The descent is a thread without safety barrier clinging to a mountainside all loose scree. I'm happy, after this pass of gloomy grandeur, to reach level ground at Mono Lake, which is deep blue and flat.

I STAY AT A MOTEL IN LEE VINING, a village of one hundred souls on the shores of Mono. The lake is fed by several rivers but has no outlet; the water evaporates as it does in the Dead Sea but it's not so saline. Swimming is possible, and there are fish—zillions of brine shrimps. Three quarters of California's gulls nest here and live on the shrimps. There is a remarkable absence of humans: it could be a tourist spot, but perhaps, like Big Sur, it's just too far from anywhere else. The lake's bird life, because people are rare, is teeming.

I lie on the lake's edge, nude. There is not one man-built thing to be seen: no fence-post, telephone pole, car, empty Coca-Cola bottle. The vegetation consists entirely of sage-brush which stretches to the horizon and beyond. A feeling of huge open spaces: distant mountains in Nevada; sky; a warm wind—the west as a pioneer might have seen it. The wind on my skin, brushing the hairs, stiffens my cock. A good place to fuck, this sandy desert. No need to check if anyone can see. I have no man with me, however.

Growing out of the lake and on the shore (the water level has dropped in recent years) are bizarre stalagmites called tufa, formed over the centuries from calceous deposits and fossilized algae. Some are twenty feet high. They give the whole region a look of moonscape or the surface of planets in science fiction's outer galaxies. A dust storm on the lake's eastern side adds to the feeling that I'm not really on Earth at all.

I travel along dirt roads to Bodie, a ghost town—I am definitely on *this* planet in a very well-preserved piece of its history. Not somewhere abandoned when the Gold Rush went sour, but a place that continued mining until 1932 when matches, carelessly struck by a small boy, caused a fire that destroyed nearly all of it. Its remoteness and punishing climate—freezing winters and scorching summers—meant that it was a very wicked town (at one time there were constant lynchings, saloon-bar brawls, stage-coach hold-ups, and a murder at least once a day) and that it changed very little in the seventy-odd years of its life. What is here now is therefore a Wild West museum: wooden Victorian houses with their simple utensils and plain furniture. One of the saloons still exists (there were sixty-five in all), so does the theatre, a church, a hotel, the bank vaults, and the school-room—complete with desks and textbooks. The theatre contains a fascinating collection of the last century's products: mining implements, domestic hardware, family photographs and letters, two funeral carriages with black plumes, and the red light from one of the many brothels. It was in Bodie that someone had the harebrained idea of rigging up wires to make electricity travel long distances. He experimented, much to the amusement of the townspeople, and it *worked*. The idea was exported to the rest of the world, so we can iron clothes more efficiently now, freeze food and see well enough to read after dark . . . and so on. Maybe it wasn't such a wicked place after all, this dinosaur.

What was it like to be gay in Bodie? Did ecstatic fucking and delicious sucking help those blizzard winter nights to pass? There is nothing in the record, of course, to show that any homosexual lived here, but . . . one in ten, one in ten. The pale stalagmites at Mono, only a few miles off, remind me of the pillar of salt on the road to Sodom.

THE TEMPERATURE IN YOSEMITE AND MONO was a pleasant mid-eighties, with a cool night wind. I left Los Gatos in mid-heatwave: a very uncomfortable one hundred and two, the house stuffy, almost stifling in the late afternoon. Even the tangerine tree looked tired. I return now to a chilly weekend in San Francisco (but a warm Phil), fog, and a thin drizzle releasing earth scents, flower scents. A hint of fall.

One may regret the fog of San Francisco summers, and agree with Mark Twain that the worst winter he ever spent was the summer he lived here. But without the Golden Gate to let in the cool moisture, this part of California would lack lungs, air conditioning, an open window to blow the staleness from a frowsty room. The Sacramento Valley would overheat, become desert, and much of the world's almond, orange, lemon, grape-fruit, peach and pear crop would not exist.

A new plague has struck the city. A bug, originating from Brazil, is killing the fuchsias, and as San Francisco is the fuchsia capital of North America, media coverage is almost as intense as it is on AIDS.

TO THE OPERA HOUSE for the Joffrey Ballet: Britten, Shos-takovich and Brahms. The Britten is *Les Illuminations*, his greatest work in my opinion. Rimbaud's poems (*and* Britten's music) constantly evoke the beauty of the male body: "Promène-toi, la nuit, en mouvant doucement cette cuisse, cette seconde cuisse et cette jambe de gauche", and these lines mean little—

> *Oh! nos os sont revêtus d'un nouveau corps amoureux.*
> *O la face cendrée, l'écusson de crin, les bras de cristal! Le canon sur lequel je dois m'abattre à travers la mêlée des arbres et de l'air léger!*

—if "canon" is not cock and "mêlée des arbres" not pubic hair. (The throbbing, hushed chords that accompany the singer here marvellously suggest the most tender love-making.)

The trouble with turning this into a ballet is that the music is so busy supporting and interpreting the poems, and the poems so deftly floating on top of the music, that dance is an intrusion—the unwanted man in a three-way, disturbing what is already perfection. It is annoying that Ashton's choreography makes not one gesture towards the homoeroticism of the words or the music, but concentrates entirely on the feverish drug-induced vision in each poem, something Britten's music plays down. Cecil Beaton's costumes—camp, witty, and looking as if they belong to a quite different ballet—only add to the confusion.

Surely the combination of Britten, Rimbaud, Ashton and Beaton could have given us a gay masterpiece! But—the date: 1950. Nobody dared to think in those terms, then.

FILOLI, HALF-WAY BETWEEN San Francisco and San José, is a neat, well-designed but essentially uninteresting mock-Georgian mansion. We are not here for the house, however; its gardens attract people in such numbers that the first available Saturday one can visit them is next October. Fortunately mid-week is less popular, but it is tedious having to join a large party on a guided tour of a garden. I want to sit on the lawn, crush herbs in my fingers, smell choisias and roses, gaze as long as I like at water lilies, hydrangeas, rudbeckias, maidenhair and tea trees, the dazzle of hibiscus and bougainvillaea. It's not allowed. Why does everything in this country have to be so *organized*?

IN SAN FRANCISCO, on the Crookedest Street in the World, I look at bougainvillaea and hydrangeas uninterrupted. On Twin Peaks see the whole city spread out for my inspection: the Bay, the bridges, Oakland, Berkeley (with its campanile visible for once), the mountains beyond. I think of the Devil taking Christ to the top of the mountain and showing him all the kingdoms, and I wonder if he would have refused this one.

I find a few bits I wrote just after I arrived in 1980. "He has white teeth, bronzed skin, sun-bleached hair." "Fire-crackers left from July the fourth festivities explode all day, all night. Until I'm told what they are, I think they are gunshots." "Every fleshly pleasure supplied, yet it has the highest suicide and alcoholism rates in the world." "An elegant Gothic church with white towers, green spires and gold weathervanes. The city is an adult's toy-box." "Too many ugly electric cables and telephone wires." "The Golden Gate Bridge—I can't believe I'm actually walking on it."

All true.

HAVE A GOOD DAY—have a good one—enjoy your day—there you go—take it easy—ya betcha—have a good trip—is that right?—well, what do ya know!—well, how about that!—Holy Smoke!—goldarnit—goddammit—durned—how ya doing?

The meaningless small change of American conversation is better than the genteel politeness of British chit-chat; it's warmer, earthier, more alive. And they think the British accent is so gorgeous; that we speak the *real* English!

Violators are towed away here (cars, not rapists), and unpaid bills "become delinquent".

On the whole the British are less welcoming, less open, less patient, less willing to help strangers. According to my experience.

But a gay bar is a gay bar is a gay bar. So is a man in one's bed, and a good fuck, and a bath-house quickie. Blessed internationalism! If cocks could speak, there would be instant Babel: thank God in every country they only want one thing—to come.

IN THE WALT WHITMAN BOOKSHOP a few weeks ago, I signed all twenty-five copies of *The Estuary* that were on sale. Every one has sold!

XVII

RENO OBSERVED FROM the California mountains is a collection of buildings dumped in the middle of a desert, and immediately prompts one to ask: what is it doing here? It's a junction—the main route west to San Francisco crosses the only highway from Oregon to Nevada and Arizona, and it was the last place of refuge before the covered wagons, en route for California, tried to cross the sierras; death, from exposure and starvation, struck the party who, instead of wintering at Reno, carried on and stopped by the Donner Lake. It's an attractive town in some ways, despite the gruelling desert temperatures and the flashy casinos; there are many pleasant Victorian houses and the park, on both sides of the Truckee River, is tree-filled and green.

People come here for the same reason they visit any town in Nevada—to take advantage of its peculiar laws: it is easier to get married or divorced here than in perhaps any other place in the civilized world; bars are open twenty-four hours a day; prostitution is legal; and, above all, gambling is not only permitted, but positively encouraged by the state government, which obtains the money it needs by taxing casinos instead of personal income. The gambling inevitably leaves its mark on the physical appearance of things—in downtown Reno casinos are more in evidence than supermarkets; hoardings that announce the benefits to be grabbed in each palace of pleasure assail the eye; and at night an enormous quantity of electricity is used by every establishment to try and upstage its competitors with a glittering display of lights and signs. The result is brash, ugly and depressing.

Inside a casino it is everlasting night. There are few windows and no clocks—the management does not want to remind the punter that it is time to go home. The decor is tasteless, the lights confusing, and the slot machines chirp unceasingly, like a million crickets, as they greedily swallow more and more coins. A casino is never empty. Where do all these men and women come from, one asks—the population of Nevada is only three quarters of a million. At Winnemucca, a town of six thousand inhabitants miles from anywhere in the desert, the night life is extraordinary—cars coming and going, crowds of people, drinking haunts and casinos packed. A place of equivalent size in England would not have a soul on its streets after 11 p.m. and it would be in darkness. The people come from all over America, of course, for there is no other state like Nevada, none that offers this kind of hedonism so brazenly and on such a scale. Arriving from California it is like being in a foreign country. No sophistication, no sense of beauty—just gaudiness and vulgarity. The landscape, too, is quite different: the sierras suddenly stop and there is desert, a not particularly interesting desert of sage-brush. History, as much as geography, accounts for the differences. Nevada was the Wild West, and it still is. It defies federal laws in a way unknown in California. It's remarkably lax, for instance, in enforcing drivers to obey the fifty-five m.p.h. speed limit; and billboards scream this or that motel or casino at you for mile after mile on its freeways. Even on remote mountain roads there is an advert for something or other to spoil nature untamed. It's as if Lady Bird Johnson's Beautification of the Highways Act had never been put on the statute book.

What, one wonders, observing a mousy middle-aged woman sweeping the floor of a casino at two o'clock in the morning, is the nature of people's private lives in Nevada? Like anywhere else? It's hard to imagine. And what is the status of religion? Nevada's first settlement was a township of Mormons, and though there are still communities of Latter-Day Saints, how was it Mormon puritanism, as an influence, died totally, whereas it still dominates neighbouring Utah?

Phil and I have come for the national gay rodeo which is held every August, and a most enjoyable weekend it turns out to be. The atmosphere in town is relaxed and welcoming—it's Reno's biggest event of the year, and the citizens ignore whatever prejudices they might have as they contemplate the money thirty to forty thousand gay people will spend in three days and three nights. Not that there are likely to be many prejudices;

we're not in Kansas or Nebraska, and Reno, small though it is, has a number of gay bars, discos and bath-houses.

Our tickets include a country and western hoedown and a barbecue. (The latter is an excellently cooked New York steak, potato salad, beans and grapes.) At the hoedown cowboys in jeans, plaid shirts, bandannas, and a variety of multi-coloured felt, leather or straw Stetsons, waltz and two-step. A hat is essential, for the daytime temperature is over a hundred degrees, so we buy a couple from one of the many booths outside the rodeo grounds. One hundred degrees: and the snow-peaked mountains are clearly visible to the west. The dancers may be Castro clones or middle-class executives who normally wear suits, but one thing in which we always excel the straights is our flair for costume: background, class, origins are hidden by the cowboy drag. It's as if a bit of history is being re-enacted, or one that never was is being created—the gay dancing which the real gay cowboy pioneers could not have indulged in.

Next morning we spend in the throng outside the rodeo grounds, drinking beer and strolling from stall to stall. All kinds of gay knick-knacks and souvenirs on sale, and pictures, pottery, jewellery, food and drink; fairground booths—throw three balls and the cute butch guy in the brief swimming costume will drop into a tub of cold water: another dollar goes to AIDS funds. Not unlike the Castro Street Fair. Then, all afternoon, the rodeo itself; thousands of gays in the stadium. I've never been to a rodeo before, and I discover—as with so many things in America that I've seen at the movies and found not quite credible—that it *is* just as it looks on celluloid. The bucking broncos buck, their rear legs rearing high in the air, and the bareback riders clutch on, defying gravity, waving their hats, and for thirty seconds become the darlings of the crowd; bulls snort and paw the ground, breathe heavily and raise the dust; cows are lassooed and kick as high as the horses; superb piebalds charge at incredible speeds: and I begin to notice one difference between the movies and this real-life spectacle—the animals usually win. Very few people get the better of them, which is as it should be; being lassooed, dragged to the ground and sat on is probably not a pleasant experience. Final score is something like gay men and women—14; cows, bulls and horses—49.

The heat is so draconian I almost faint. But all afternoon dark clouds like bruises build over the mountains; by evening a strong hot wind is blowing in off the desert, and there is a lurid sunset—all shades of pink, orange and purple staining the edges of the clouds. A storm seems very likely, but it does not happen. We drink in various bars, meet other gay couples, and eventually go in a crowd to a disco that doesn't look promising—it's a long way out of town, virtually in the desert. But it's the best disco we've been to for months, real *Night Fever* stuff: we can actually dance. Poppers in an enormous bottle on the counter, courtesy of the management. Some beautiful cowboys.

FROM RENO TO VIRGINIA CITY, which is not quite a ghost town, for seven hundred people live here; once there were twenty-five thousand. Gold greed began it and fire ended it, as in Bodie—but the history of the two places is very different. Despite the man who discovered that electricity could be made to travel long distances, Bodie was brutish and nasty; in Virginia City one could be piss-elegant. The world's largest vein of gold—the Comstock Lode—was found here, and as a result Virginia City had an opera house, twenty theatres, a hotel which boasted the biggest elevator west of Chicago, a railroad, Mark Twain, the first telephones in the West—and a tradition of culture. One can still drink in saloons which have their original counters, mirrors and decor, and buy groceries in stores unchanged in a century. The train, complete with whistle, huge chimney and cowcatcher, still operates. The life-styles of the present inhabitants, however, clash badly with what they are trying to preserve. Cars are allowed on Main Street, and, being Nevada, the inevitable slot machines abound. Every house is privately owned; high prices are charged for the viewing of each little bit of the past and tawdry souvenirs are offered to the tourist. Even so, it's possible to immerse oneself in the feel of the place and be astonished, as at Bodie, that history so recent can be utterly unlike now. We don't see this in Britain: our nineteenth century is not far away—so much of it we live with and use. In the West of America some of it is as antique as the

Pyramids because life here has changed so quickly and so totally.

IN CARSON CITY WE LOOK at Nevada's capitol, a diminutive building for a state legislature, about the size of San Francisco's public library. Nothing much of interest here: old maps and portraits of gloomy Governors. Little of Nevada's history, no clues to the oddity of its laws, no explanation of how the city got its name. When we emerge we find it's been raining. There is a lovely smell of wet grass and petunias.

Over the mountains to Tahoe; more storm clouds, and the lake is steely grey. Pine forests. Summer cabins. Deserted ski-slopes. It's three months since I was here and there was twenty feet of snow on the ground: all gone. The lake is so big that it's easy to avoid the tourists and enjoy the scenery, but the inhabited southern end is dreadful. There are two towns—Stateline, Nevada, and South Lake Tahoe, California—but they run into each other and are, in effect, one. South Lake Tahoe doesn't have Stateline's hideous casinos, but it's an awful example of the worst kind of ribbon development—shoddy souvenir shops, ugly motels, and cheap bad restaurants, all plonked down in some of the most beautiful landscape imaginable.

TALES OF THE CITY by Armistead Maupin is a volume of short stories that originally appeared in the *SF Chronicle*. It's an affectionate, accurate, and sometimes caustic portrait of San Francisco. Gay life in particular comes over effectively—warts and all. Amusing, too, are the frustrations of hetero Brian, dishy and sex-starved, who has considerable problems in finding women to fuck, and, when he does, problems in persuading them that he is not gay. It reminds one of the corny joke about how many straight men are required here to screw in a light bulb: answer—both of them. Or the rhyme on some tee-shirts in Castro clothes shops:

> *Come to San Francisco City*
> *Where the women are strong and the men are pretty.*

Tales of the City was published in 1978 and was followed by

[122]

More Tales of the City (the same recipe, but not quite so funny), then *Further Tales of the City*, in which the whole idea grows a bit threadbare. The *Chronicle* is currently doing a fourth series, even though the wit has lost its edge, cliché is strong in every sentence, and the characters have become so two-dimensional that their reactions and comments are tediously predictable. Michael, who is gay, is visiting London—and *Chronicle* readers therefore now get a weekly dose of misinformation about British gay life. Examples: Michael can buy *Gay News*, though it ceased to exist four months ago; reads a paper called *Capital and Gay*; is unaware of the Champion, though he's living in Notting Hill and bought *Gay News* to check on the pubs; and finds Harpoon Louie's a stone's throw from the Coleherne and just like an American bar. Most irritating of all, because it perpetuates a myth common in the States, Maupin's tales depict London as very shabby and dirty, and the Brits—paralysed by roaring inflation, unemployment and a weak pound—as poverty-stricken and depressing: the clones, for instance, in the Coleherne are a sad, pale reflection of their mighty brothers on Castro Street.

San Francisco is one of the worst cities I know for litter and dog shit, and Americans, it seems to me, have just as much, or as little, money to spend as we have. I haven't found a United States groaning with unparalleled affluence.

RECENT RESEARCH SHOWS that if pregnant rats are subjected to severe stress the male rats that are born will behave like females. The head of the Institute for Experimental Endocrinology in East Berlin, Dr Dorner, says that this is how human homosexuality is created. He interviewed two hundred gay men born during the Second World War and found that seventy per cent of their mothers had had moderately or severely stressful pregnancies. The *San Francisco Examiner and Chronicle* devotes a whole page to this rubbish, and though it doesn't go so far as to suggest that Dr Dorner is right, it implies that he could be.

Several basic points of common sense are ignored here: they seem so obvious that they are hardly worth mentioning. But should this diary fall into the hands of a neanderthal straight—or gay—here they are:

[123]

1. How does Dr Dorner account for the homosexuality of the thirty per cent whose mothers had no history of stress during pregnancy?

2. A survey of two hundred people is so small that it can't claim for itself any reliable scientific truth.

3. If Dr Dorner had interviewed two hundred straight men in the Second World War, he would probably have found, considering what was happening at the time, that seventy per cent of them also had mothers whose pregnancies were moderately or severely stressful.

4. It is quite absurd to think that human homosexuality in males has anything to do with being female. A man who likes to fuck another man is not indulging in an activity that could be called, in any sense of the word, "female".

Dr Dorner says his gender-bewildered rats lacked testosterone because of their mothers' stressful pregnancies, and that it may be possible to "correct such abnormalities" in humans with testosterone injections before we are born. Thus providing the gay "problem", I suppose, with a Final Solution.

If all homosexual men were testosterone deficient, we'd have high voices, no chest hair, no baldness . . . and we'd probably all want to get fucked.

AIDS HYSTERIA NOW in the British press: an article in the *Observer* says that thousands of British gays could already have the disease, but, because of the long incubation period, they don't know it. Presumably they've caught it from Americans— I've heard of the Special Relationship, but I didn't realize Anglo–American fucking was so extensive. Much of the information seems to derive from *Newsweek*'s sober and well-written account, but there is one amusing inaccuracy. The *Observer* says that most at risk are those gays who have a thousand or more sexual contacts each year—in other words, sex with three different men every single day! More likely to die of physical exhaustion, I would imagine. The *Newsweek* article said a thousand or more in a *life-time*.

CHECK-OUT IN AN AMERICAN SUPERMARKET is much more pleasant than in Liptons or Sainsburys. The girl actually speaks *and* puts all the groceries in bags for you. If the queue is long you can read the various papers on offer. You're supposed to buy them, but nobody in their right senses would do so—sample headlines: "Ted Will Marry Jackie To Make Sure Of White House", "Queen Lets Andrew Marry Koo", "I Had A Space Alien's Baby". It makes *Paris Match* seem the soul of rectitude.

If the pregnancies of Martians and Prince Andrew's sex life do not appeal, there are magazines full of articles on how to make your body beautiful or how to improve your own sex life. One of these reports that a group of British men managed, during a period of about four hours, to make their cocks permanently bigger by as much as two inches. What methods were used, and whether the organs were flaccid or erect, was not revealed. Any withdrawal symptoms, I wonder?

XVIII

HARRIET, DREADING LONELINESS, does all the wrong things—
as most of us would, I imagine, after the collapse of an affair of
nearly twenty years' duration. The Corona Corona monk has
been wining and dining her again, and showering her with
expensive presents. He's at the monastery, he says, to keep an
eye on Los Gatos, to protect us from all the murderers and
rapists in the community. (We have in fact had one murder
this summer—a woman chopped her husband up and buried
him in their garden.) Alarmed by what she sees as crazy boast-
fulness, Harriet gets very cool, but this only encourages the mad
monk all the more. He phones at 3 a.m. to tell her to make
certain her doors are locked; there are two escaped prisoners on
the loose. Which is true—he probably obtained the information
from the radio. Nothing could be more calculated to distress a
woman living alone, of course. He is able to give her a detailed
account of exactly what she has been doing in the past week:
what restaurant she lunched in, where she turned off the freeway to do her shopping, etcetera. She is terrified, she says, of
being strangled in the middle of the night by this obvious
nutter. What should she do? Go to the Jesuits and/or to the
police, Katya and I tell her—the man is dotty, probably harmless . . . but you can't be sure. At the very least, he's a considerable nuisance. But she is disinclined to seek help from the
authorities. Because—it occurs to me—she's either making it
up, or exaggerating it out of all proportion, so that Katya will
take pity on her and move into her house. Harriet has mounted a
strong campaign in that direction in recent weeks; her offers,
however, have fallen on stony ground.

She eventually stops badgering Katya, and at much the same
time we hear no more about the mad monk. Then she decides
she needs a psychiatrist, who turns out to be gay and also at the

end of a long affair. Their sessions together consist more of the psychiatrist unburdening herself than Harriet doing so. The upshot—Harriet takes in, as a tenant, the psychiatrist's ex-lover, who has two dogs and smokes. (Harriet cannot abide cigarette smoke—when it suits her.)

Sarah has also consulted a psychiatrist, but seems to be coping a little more successfully. She spent much of the vacation on the East Coast with a young lesbian teaching assistant, and is looking fit, thinner, and suntanned. But with tigerish nervous energy. She returns to Harriet's to collect some of her property, but instead of just packing up quickly and leaving, she gets involved in a heated argument that rages on all day. I go up there to help Sarah move out a bed, and I hear their voices screaming as I turn into the drive. Just like old times.

Katya, who left her second husband and divorced him after twenty-six years of marriage, did *not* rush into doing all the wrong things. She has the love and loyalty of her children, and leads a social life so hectic it makes me feel exhausted. She has spurned psychiatrists, rows with her ex-husbands, singles bars, unsuitable partners; and in consequence she is not plagued with mad monks or chain-smoking lesbians. Her worst moments are waking up in the small hours and being without that other life in the bed beside her: but she knows quite well that the silliest course of action after break-up is to look for an instant replacement.

TO THEATRE ON THE SQUARE with Phil, for Harvey Fierstein's three one-act plays, *Torch Song Trilogy*—winner of this year's Tony Award, and much admired by critics, gay and straight. We find it too long, not funny, all words and no action, and nearly every line is a put-down of gay life. It's written by a gay man and it's about gay men, but it's full of unliberated self-mockery. The central character is a professional drag queen—that known and loved (by straights) gay symbol. The audience, mostly straight, enjoyed it, of course. We left after the second play, and had more fun drinking coffee and eating macaroons at Häagen-Dazs on Castro.

I am really puzzled that gay critics and all my gay friends like it. Can't they see the self-oppression in limp-wristed mincing humour? How it reinforces the stereotype, and helps to keep us where the world wants us? Gives "proof" to Dr Dorner?

Something similar is at work in the success of the musical version of *La Cage aux Folles*, which has just opened on Broadway. If gays can be seen only as men dressed as women, then the straight world feels unthreatened; it can laugh us off. *The Naked Civil Servant*, recently on TV here, is also insidious. Of course John Hurt's performance is marvellous, but isn't Quentin Crisp for much of the time portrayed as a sad, pathetic failure? The episodes in bed are the most unerotic I've ever seen. Isn't it easy for the straight to deduce from this that a gay fuck is unfulfilling, second best? And that gay men are long-haired effeminate poufs; women, really, but alas in male bodies? I doubt if *The Naked Civil Servant* would have been half so popular if Quentin Crisp had been a macho construction worker who lusted after dishy young blonds.

POINT REYES OUGHT TO BE AN ISLAND. It was once, and it will be again, though not in my life-time. It belongs to the Pacific plate, but aeons ago it hit the American continent and has been more or less attached to California ever since, though the 1906 earthquake knocked it a whole twenty feet north. It's a wild, remote area of sand-dunes, marsh and sea-grasses, not unlike the Suffolk coast near Aldeburgh and Southwold. The final tip of the point, thin and craggy, is a mere footpath wide; there is a churning sea and a lighthouse I can glimpse only infrequently through the rushing fog, hundreds of feet below.

A huge grey head, a long way off, surfaces; then a flash of vast tail fins. I have never seen a whale before.

We sit on a beach, Phil, me, Janos and Jim, in the fog, and spend hours drinking Almadén and talking about life.

THE CASTRO STREET FAIR ONCE MORE. Which means I've been in California just over a year. Nothing to say of the fair that I didn't say at the beginning of this diary. The crowds are bigger. Same drag queens, leather clones, imitation nuns. The stalls are still selling everything nobody wants to buy—imitation feather boas, imitation stained glass. Left over from last year, most likely.

[128]

I didn't end up this time fucking a polite Chinese. But I enjoyed myself, just the same, seeing it all with Phil.

SARAH WINCHESTER (1842–1922) was as batty as a fruitcake. Her only child died at the age of six weeks, and a short while afterwards she lost her husband, from whom she inherited the Winchester Rifle fortune: it earned her as much as a thousand dollars a day. Her widowhood lasted forty-two years, and during that time she communed regularly with the spirits of her husband and daughter, who persuaded her that her money was accursed. In order to atone, they said, she had to build a mansion big enough to house all the spirits of the people shot dead by the Winchester Rifle; to avoid dying herself, she should keep the builders at work twenty-four hours a day, every day of the year. She did just that.

Winchester House, San José's most spectacular monument, is a bizarre Victorian folly, and consists literally of hundreds of rooms, staircases and corridors. Some of the stairs lead no-where—they stop at walls and ceilings. Cupboard doors open, but there may be no cupboards; revealed on the other side is, for example, an eight-foot drop into a kitchen sink in the room below. The house was severely damaged in the 1906 earth-quake, which was caused, Sarah believed, by herself not build-ing quickly enough. She redoubled her efforts, but outwards instead of upwards. (The top three floors collapsed in 1906.) Rooms that were partly destroyed were shut up and left in disrepair (no one knows why) and can be seen to this day, exactly as they were after the great jolting.

She was an almost total recluse, and saw nobody except for her twenty servants and the builders. It sounds like a conscience so guilty (for rather ill-defined reasons) that the personality, in order to survive, retreats into a kind of harmless derangement. One cannot say that she wasted her money, even though the vast majority of those rooms were never used; she has given pleasure to millions of tourists ever since and thus, ironically, earned the immortality the spirits said would be hers if she did what they told her to do.

The house is built in that same exquisite Victorian good taste that makes San Francisco such a delight, but the unnecessary

over-organization that is part of a visit to most American historical monuments destroys all sense of atmosphere. You can't be
left alone for a second; a guided tour must be taken, and three
howling babies are included on mine. There is a dreadful gift
shop with space-invader machines, and all over the garden
loudspeakers blare out folksy reminiscences by Mrs
Winchester's surviving employees. Tacky!

I OBTAIN COPIES OF THE MEDICAL RECORDS of my illness—
how open America is compared with Britain! I cannot imagine
being allowed to read a doctor's notes and a specialist's report in
Exeter. My fever, my headaches and my large quantities of
protein, it appears, were of little interest to the doctors, and it's
nice to know that my brain, eyes, ears, nose, throat, lungs,
heart, genitals and so on are "normal". Nice, too, to be
described as a "well-developed" male. Which part of the
anatomy were they thinking of? What did interest the doctors
was the peculiar state of my blood. I had leukopenia, neutro-
penia, thrombocytopenia, lymphocytosis, a sedimentation rate
of six (twenty is usual) and a count of seventy-six thousand
platelets (instead of the customary two hundred and sixteen
thousand.) Which suggests too many lymphocytes, not enough
white corpuscles, and something like haemophilia. The doctors
weren't sure this was viral in origin. The final blood test showed
everything as it should be, except for an excessive quantity of
lymphocytes. (A blood test, taken a year later, however, showed
that the production of lymphocytes had returned to normal.)
What on earth does it all mean?

WHAT'S UP DOC? second time round is nothing like so funny.
It's just a bit too mad and improbable, though the car chases
remain some of the best of all time. Streisand and O'Neall are
not brilliant at any point: the star of the show is Madeline Kahn
as O'Neall's neurotic fiancée—she *is* funny. And convincing. I
saw it before I ever came to San Francisco, so wanted to see it
again for locations I now know so well. My memory has
deceived me; very little of the film takes place out of doors, and
what there is of the city flashes by so fast that, with the exception of a few obvious shots of the Crookedest Street in the

World, Chinatown and a token cable car, it's impossible to know if we're on Powell, Hyde, Leavenworth—it could be a steep hill anywhere.

IN A BAR ON CASTRO I MEET CHUCK, a twenty-two-year-old blond. It's a hot evening; we're drinking outside on the terrace, and he's stripped to the waist. A light dusting of gold hair on his suntanned chest. White, white teeth. Brown eyes that look both young and very defiant. He's from New York, but went to Atlanta where he graduated. There he decided to come out as gay, and he fell in love with the first man he ever had sex with. But this man couldn't, or wouldn't, offer the monogamous "marriage" Chuck desired, so, hurt, he left and came to San Francisco. He has been in the city a month, washing dishes in a restaurant and living in a dilapidated room on Polk.

"I don't see why a gay relationship shouldn't be exactly like a heterosexual marriage," he says. He hopes to find the lover of his dreams here. In four weeks he's made about thirty acquaintances, no friends, and not found love—just sex; one-night stands and three-ways.

Physically I'm his ideal, he tells me—the moustache, the dark hair, the fit muscular body. The high cheek-bones. And he just loves my British accent.

Physically he's *my* ideal, too. And I'm attracted to (and appalled by) that wide-eyed innocence: so many gay kids, injured by hostile families and environments, come here, hoping the streets are paved with gold. Castro will hurt him more than the guy in Atlanta—I'd like to protect him from that. I can't, of course. I don't even suggest we spend the night together, much as I'd love it. It would only add to his hurt. I wish him well, say I hope he finds what he wants, and kiss him goodbye.

He's imposing his own private vision of things on the city, and you cannot do that: he has a long journey before he discovers some truths about love, sex and "marriage".

UP IN THE HILLS, behind the monastery. As it was when I was first here: fall light, pink belladonna lilies in flower, shiny poison oak, hot fumes of fennel, dusty grasses withered as dead sticks. Eucalyptus scents. Eucalyptus trees look unnatural—

their flaky bark reveals a smooth polished wood like furniture, and their leaves are torpid bats hanging, or rags left on washing-lines. Flies bite here. My skin, albeit delectably bronzed, is in bad condition—dry and wrinkly from too much sun, and it's scarred with old fly bites, months old, that refuse to heal. Birds whirr unexpectedly out of the bushes, and lizards scuttle, the rustle of their movements as dry as the stones and the dust. Today is windy, so there is no fog or smog and I can see downtown San Francisco and the Bay Bridge, sixty miles off. The skyscrapers are faint grey pencil etchings. San José is its usual evergreens and Delphic columns, and the Santa Clara Mountains are, of course, as if basted in the ovens of the sun.

I shall miss all this. Tomorrow is September; in three weeks I shall be back in England.

XIX

THE FINAL BIG TRIP, looking for Gary. Spearfish in Las Vegas.
I cross the Sonora Pass to Mono, then drive south. The high
sierras are on my right, their peaks still covered with snow
which will not melt now before the winter storms begin. They
are great jagged grey faces of bare granite, their contours clear in
the September morning, but blue and hazy at dusk. Once more
I can look at Mount Whitney, then Owens Lake which dried up
centuries ago and left a barren salt-pan: such a contrast is
uncommon anywhere else in the world—except in England.
One can travel three hundred miles in England and cross several
totally different kinds of landscape. So it is here: from Mono to
Lone Pine where I turn east and leave the sierras is many varied
countries. The stalagmites of Mono, then volcanoes remarkably
like the volcanoes children draw—steep sides and jagged
craters—but, though it seems they could erupt at any moment
because the ash on their slopes looks so fresh, there is no smoke
swirling out. From here to Bishop is pine forest. After that alfalfa
fields and I stop in an attempt to find elks: the largest herd in
California grazes here, by the shores of Lake Tinemaha. But
there are no elks. It's the rutting season, and it's also very hot;
they're probably in the shade of the distant trees—rutting. A
rare bird, a roadrunner, hops across the track, not at all
bothered that I'm so near. I drive on, through sage-brush and
sand, to Independence, and at Lone Pine there is the Owens salt
lake-bed. Five landscapes in a hundred and twenty miles.

In Lone Pine I lose a hundred dollars; between paying a
restaurant bill and walking to a bar across the street, a roll of
twenties vanishes from my pocket. I spend a long time search-
ing, but it's been spirited away. Someone, doubtless, is raving it
up this Saturday night at my expense. I sleep badly, annoyed by
the loss and interrupted by rowdy couples returning to their

motel rooms at 3, 4, 5 a.m. In the next bedroom several people fuck all night long. The walls shake with the heaving of buttocks and the thrashing of limbs, and as the sperm erupts the pants and moans are as loud as blast-furnaces.

On, to Death Valley. The vegetation thins—pickleweed and Mormon tea: it's too hostile even for sage-brush. Greyish-yellow earth. Dust. Suddenly, the descent. Canyons open on either side of the road, huge clefts lurching down for hundreds of feet. Black volcanic rock, and rock the colour of the minerals deposited there, a dull red, a poisonous pink. The road is dangerous—hairpin bends and sheer falls. At the bottom is Panamint Springs—two or three houses, a gas station and a café, both closed. Springs? There is no water. The valley is all sand; the road crosses it as the crow flies, then twists up the pass through the Panamint Mountains. I'm not in Death Valley yet. That's on the far side of the Panamints, which are just about the most impressive and inhospitable mountains I have ever seen, a huge barrier of utterly barren grey rock that rises from below sea level to eleven thousand feet, inimical, desolate, sun-punished, awesome. I think they are quite amazingly beautiful.

But the Townes Pass through the Panamints is gentle and, if there were no road, if one were on foot, it would be easy enough to traverse. I say that because in 1849 a party of gold-seekers, coming from Utah and looking for a short cut, entered Death Valley and could not find a way out through the Panamints. Their story is haunting and tragic. For a month they lived on the floor of the valley, which is consistently the hottest place on earth, and has the dubious honour of having the highest temperature ever recorded—one hundred and thirty-four degrees in the shade—and it is virtually without water. There are no living things here, or so the forty-niners said, no birds, animals, fish. It's not quite true; they meant no *edible* things. They killed their oxen for food, burned their wagons, and made their way out of the valley on foot, not west through the Panamints, but south. Only one of them died in Death Valley, but many perished afterwards as they walked on. Why didn't they turn back? The desire to get to the gold before anyone else?

The descent from the Townes Pass is not troublesome, and the views are spectacular. Death Valley, one can see, is many kinds of desert—walls of rock on either side, but the bottom is sand-dune, scrub, salt, stone, and it changes quickly from one to another, minute by minute as I drive. Stovepipe Wells, five feet above sea level, is a store, a gas station, and a motel. The temperature here is one hundred and nineteen degrees, and it's not yet mid-day. I buy some beer and drink it in the sun, enjoying the heat on my skin. Then go on, into the sand-dunes; stop the car and walk for a while. There *is* life here. In the sand are the curious S-shapes left by sidewinder snakes, like hieroglyphics or masons' marks that, one thinks, would mean something urgent if only one could decode them.

At Furnace Creek there is a museum: a building that resembles a modern high school, surrounded by very green grass. It seems quite absurd that it exists, with its irrigation, air conditioning and drinking fountains, and I wish it didn't, for it somehow suggests that humans could, if they wanted to, make Death Valley look like anywhere else. Not far away are the ruins of the Harmony Borax Mine. That anyone should have found it profitable to mine anything in Death Valley is incomprehensible, considering the climate and the need to use twenty-mule teams to transport the stuff one hundred and fifty miles to Mojave, the nearest rail-head, across some of the most formidable terrain in the world. The miners were mainly Chinese. Perhaps they were thought to be more dispensable than whites.

Zabriskie Point, where Antonioni filmed all those naked young couples making love in the sand, is a different landscape again—dried yellow mud, a model of an uninhabitable planet's surface, folds and canyons and waterless streams wriggling downwards into the valley. I take off all my clothes and sunbathe for an hour. The heat is kiln-like and the silence absolute.

At Dante's View I'm five thousand feet up, and the drop is almost perpendicular. It's cool and refreshing here—a mere ninety degrees. There are all the Panamints, from below sea level to the towering summit of Telescope Peak. Beyond, the snow of the sierras. On the bottom is a lake, Bad Water, undrinkable and white in colour; the dried-up bed of the Armagosa River; sand; petrified salt deposits and the crunchy salt crystals of the Devil's Golf Course; other dust I can't put a name to, a kind of hideous bright green. Yes, Dante's vision of hell. If landscape has meaning, symbol, significance, rather than just simply *is*, it has it in this desert. This is the country of our nightmares. Our mistiest and most irrational fears have shape in Death Valley: a putrid smell, for example, or a sick taste of metal, neither of which I can explain, is expressed in that hideous bright green. There are no clouds, no birds drifting on wind currents, no sign of any creature, alive or dead. The silence is thick and it reverberates as in an empty cathedral at nightfall: it engulfs me against my will, deprives me of my knowledge of myself as a warm, living human animal. It is my own mortality I'm experiencing—this is despair, negation, the inevitable not-me to come.

THE NAMES OF DEATH VALLEY PLACES record the mortality other men have felt here: Furnace Wash, Dry Mountain, Funeral Peak, the Devil's Cornfield, Starvation Canyon.

Death Valley Junction is a ghost town. In the doorway of a derelict house an old woman sits on a rocking-chair, a rifle on her lap. Behind her, two Dobermann Pinschers are barking malevolently. She doesn't answer my request for water, just raises the rifle slightly; I feel it's prudent to leave. Death Valley Junction is modern, unlike most California ghost towns; there is even a ruined gas station. And an opera house! Here, in the middle of the desert, is the Armagosa Opera House. Its walls inside are covered in murals, obviously painted in recent years. What mad folly led to the building of this place? What is its story? The only person who could tell me is the old woman with the rifle, but I'm not happy about the gun or the dogs. I drive away without solving the mystery.

At the Nevada state-line is the usual casino, though I'm still in the desert and there isn't another house in sight. I drink vast quantities of water, orange juice and beer.

THOUGH PEOPLE COME TO BOTH PLACES, Las Vegas is, like Death Valley, antagonistic to most forms of human life. It's an excrescence on the middle of an extremely uninteresting desert: its buildings are ugly, and it lacks Reno's trees and grass. Its daytime temperatures in summer are consistently over one hundred and they rarely fall below eighty at night. The air is humid and smog-polluted. To observe Las Vegas at a distance is to see a cloud of a peculiarly unpleasant mauve colour.

It exists for only one reason—to prey on human greed. Downtown Las Vegas, like Reno, is not shops, offices and public monuments, but hotels, motels, and casinos. My first reaction to the famous strip where most of the big casinos are to be found is sheer disbelief. I have never seen such glittering light. After a few minutes I walk away, then return, thinking my eyes must have made some curious mistake. They haven't; the second viewing produces the same sensation of protest at one's senses. The strip is all the world's fairgrounds put together and seen at once. Piccadilly Circus is a pygmy in comparison. I am bombarded with flashing colours and dazzling brilliance as every casino tries to out-scream its neighbour in advertising its existence. It is all undoubtedly rather beautiful.

There is nothing else that is beautiful in Las Vegas. The interiors of the casinos are a barrage of electricity and sound; the bulbs glare, the bells jangle, and the slot machines shriek raucously as they chew up quarters and dimes. There are crowds of people everywhere, gambling, gambling, gambling. The employees for the most part seem so pale and tired they look like grubs asleep. There is something *bad* about this city.

To lure you inside, each casino offers an extra attraction that will devalue those announced by its rivals. You can make a free phone call to anywhere in the United States; or drink as many free strawberry daquiris as you like; have a free photograph of yourself, a key-ring embossed with your initials, or your name in a newspaper headline—"David Rees Queen of Red Lights", for example. All of them serve food and alcohol very inexpensively. Las Vegas must be one of the world's bargains for eating and drinking—vodka and orange for half a dollar, breakfast for seventy-five cents, New York steak for a couple of bucks.

In which casino is Gary waiting on tables?

I eat an excellent dinner that costs a mere four dollars, and I have not one but two waiters dancing attendance. A listless, dispirited girl, and a very beautiful young man. He has pale straw-blond hair, splendid white teeth, and eyes of the deepest blue. Almost Oriental cheek-bones. His body, in tight-fitting clothes, looks lean and energetic. About six feet tall. Is it him?

There's something familiar, yes, but this boy is much better-looking, sexier, more . . . more sure of himself than Gary's photos—or his correspondence and phone calls—implied. We talk; he graduated this May and he's working here through the summer. Tonight is his last night, thank God, and he can leave this hell-hole.

"Where are you going?" I ask.

"Dallas."

"Gary?"

He looks puzzled. "Yes? Do I know you?"

"David."

The girl brings my bill. On the back she has written "Meet me at 2 a.m. when I've finished work—Joyce." I look at her, astonished, as she scurries away to the kitchen. Then I laugh—out of embarrassment, I suppose.

"I told her she'd have no luck," Gary says. "And that was before I knew who you were."

In my king-size motel bed. His body is without blemish; it is perfection. Unlike the other casino employees, he's suntanned, all over, not a white patch anywhere. The hair on his legs and the pubic hair are golden; the pecs are superbly developed, the curve of the biceps firm, the thighs equally firm and muscular. His cock is a good hard eight inches or more. He lies on his back, one leg bent, one arm under his head. And smiles.

XX

ALL CREATIVE WRITING IS SELECTIVE, even a diary. There is
another diary I could have written, its theme my year as visiting
professor at a California university. To compare the teaching
methods, administration, expectations, successes and failures
of English departments in academic institutions in the New
World and the Old is, I guess, a worthwhile concern; David
Lodge in *Changing Places* wrote a highly readable comic novel
about it. I've said almost nothing of my colleagues or my
students, and other areas of my life have not found much space
in this attempt to turn a year into words—my reading (I read
about a hundred and twenty books all told), my daily routine at
the gym in Campbell and the people I met there, the characters
of my friends and my relationships with them, and Katya's
children with whom I spent much more time than I've suggested. I can't imagine why a sophisticated, gregarious Russian
emigré, perfectly attuned to the American West, should want to
spend a whole year in a remote part of Ireland, but in February
Katya will be coming to live in Galway. So I shall see her. And
Phil; I've recorded more of my feelings of detachment from him
than my feelings of attachment to him, but they, the latter, are
probably too private even for a diary. Or maybe I can't, or don't
want to, imprison those feelings in words. He arrives in Exeter
on Christmas Eve and will be with me for a month. I am not yet
certain, but I may break several laws to bring him here for good.

Words written in consecutive phrases and sentences have
their own structures and logical associations, illogical under-
tones and meanings, different from the structures of the
thoughts that beget them, and are outside the control the writer
would like to exercise over them. They are particularly poor
pieces of equipment for dealing with our profoundest convic-
tions and emotional experiences. So, love becomes the most

difficult word in the English language to define. (The second most difficult, I often think, is pornography.) It is easier for me to put into words the appearance of a mountain or a lake and how it affects me, though it isn't because it's a soft option that this diary concentrates on scenery, a sense of place—and music, the male body, sex. The sifting process has not been all that conscious, even if I, as a gay man in San Francisco in the 1980s, think it important to discuss what I see of gay life in that city, and, equally, feel it of dubious value to preserve my conversations in bed with a waif from the Vietnamese boats, the thoughts and emotions, the history and geography, that his words and his body convey to me.

He and I had this in common for a year: we were jetsam in a society that perhaps more than any other consists of jetsam; he, tossed east across the Pacific by the horrors and consequences of war, I, just simply attracted to Gay Mecca. Neither of us totally lost a sense of transience or detachment from the land in which we'd arrived, though he, perhaps more than I, wanted to. However, that uneasy awareness of impermanence is also the heady sniff of freedom, and never before have I experienced that so strongly as in California. Free from the restraints of my usual responsibilities, I did, except for my twelve hours a week at the university, exactly what I chose to do. I enjoyed sex with men of all races and colours of skin to a degree that is, I guess, impossible in Britain; I experienced landscape of a vastness and grandeur unknown in Europe; and explored cities as ugly or as beautiful as, but quite different from, those in our cluttered countries.

What, after all, is California; how do I sum it up? I can't begin to put it in words with any kind of adequacy. Mentally, my California doesn't even follow the real borders of the Golden State: I know almost nothing of the north with its giant redwood forests, or the southern deserts where it touches Mexico. My California seems to embrace most of Nevada and Utah, and something of Arizona. Its frontier begins just north of San Francisco and travels east to include Reno and Salt Lake City, then turns south, dips round the Grand Canyon, and ends on the Pacific somewhere between Los Angeles and San Diego. Beyond that frontier is the wrinkled surface of a continent I know little about—it's merely land I have crossed. My California doesn't contain the peculiar religions and weird cults that have sprouted in recent decades, mind-expanding drugs, flower power, student revolution, freaks and fads and fetishes; its artists, writers and musicians; the movies, silicon chips and soft fruit by which it earns its income; the ordinary, nine-to-five routine existence that over twenty-two million of its twenty-three million inhabitants are said to live. My California is certain cities, deserts, mountains, music, people, solitude.

What are David's books about, somebody once asked a friend of mine, who replied: "Sex, scenery, and Sibelius." Perhaps, then, I've not learned so much, or been changed less by California than I'd thought; perhaps this diary is the mixture as before, the result of doing what I said Chuck was wrong to attempt: imposing my own vision on the things I've seen and experienced.

Why the sex? some readers will say. Why record all those orgasms and big cocks? Where does the heaving, thrusting, licking, sucking get us? There is a strictly limited number of copulatory positions and surely we all know them and frequently use them? Isn't the whole bath-house syndrome a frantic and futile search for romance with the perfect stranger that results in ignoring the potential of the relationships I already have? No. Nor is it to titillate, or work out hang-ups, or wank while I type. Some may react with jealousy, or even puritanical shock; and there will be those who feel, perhaps because they are defensive about their bodies or those of their lovers, that gay writing should not be concerned with beautiful flesh. There is also the danger of boring the reader. I found much of John Rechy's *The Sexual Outlaw* tedious; the first time the narrator said "He put his cock in my mouth" I was certainly interested to know what happened next, but, by the thirty-ninth occasion, I wished he was describing some other object he'd put in his mouth, such as the egg he'd eaten at breakfast. But John Rechy's book deals with two very important facts we should remember. For centuries we have not been permitted to write about gay sex; now we can—and therefore we should try. Also Rechy tells us that being gay

[141]

isn't *primarily* about relationships, politics, adopting certain life-styles or codes of ethics: being gay is essentially making love with people of one's own sex. And he's right.

No other subject interests us so much; we think about it, talk about it, and do it as often as we can. In our fantasies we rehearse perfect men to fuck with, and picture them in the pages of the books we read. And for me there was something else of just as much consequence. As a bit of jetsam in that jetsam society I was, in some ways, very fragile. In California I was much more aware than at any time, before or since, of my own impermanence, of that one fact of which I can be sure—my death. It was not just a feeling produced by a serious illness, earthquakes, the *momento mori* of Death Valley, fear of AIDS, the seeming insubstantiality of cities built on fault-lines, the possibility of being shot dead on the streets. Nor was it simply the absence of my own four walls in Exeter with their windows on to the hills and the cathedral towers, my attic workroom to which I retreat as into a dark warm cave that is wholly mine and of my own creation—solid, reassuring, with its copies of my published books, that couple of feet of print (that nobody, afterwards, may read them doesn't bother me) which is my two fingers to the inevitable not-me to come. It was all of this, but more. To be in California is to be conscious of past and present in a wholly different way from in Europe, to know one's utter insignificance in the great time-continuum. Our visible European past is mostly man-made things that comfort and console us—churches, works of art, old houses; it is not at all the same sensation to walk in a desert unchanged since before man was, or to stand against the trunk of a tree two thousand seven hundred years old. The desert, the sequoia, may be beautiful—but they certainly remind one of one's slenderness in a way the *Mona Lisa* or the *Choral Symphony* do not. Set against the uncaring permanence of landscapes are freeways and cities and people often so instant, so new, so much illustrations of the dictum that the hazards California faces today America—and the rest of the world—must meet tomorrow that it is no surprise one sees oneself and those who live here as awash between then, now, and finally. Sex, therefore, takes on a new importance—it becomes a recoil from fragility. Warm, living, human animals, indulging in the experience that brings more pleasure and satisfaction than any other, are agreeing—if only for a few minutes—that skin, muscle and cock are not mortal, not nearer to death . . . but alive, alive. And the Vietnamese, the black, the Filipino, the Yugoslav, the Australian, the Latino, the Canadian in my bed are telling me I am of all mankind, that every man's life enhances me, not that every man's death diminishes me.

I CONCLUDE THIS DIARY AS I BEGAN IT, preoccupied with a better class of blond. A friend of mine said, a few years ago when I was depressed about something—or someone—"Think blond." He wasn't just talking of fair hair. Jean Genet once said he had been asked to write a play about blacks, but it was difficult: first of all you had to decide what colour they were. Again, I know what is meant—these words that signify colour of skin or hair may suggest other physical attributes, mental attitudes, emotions, history, place. So, though Gary in the literal sense is blond, Phil, dark-haired and olive-skinned, is metaphorically, and therefore *really*, blond: lover. So words slip, slide, perish under the strain we put on them—or become pregnant with meaning. "California" is another example.

I only said what he looked like naked; I could have said what we talked about, what I thought of him, how he was coping with his father's death. He was nice enough, not so very different from the impression his letters and phone calls had given me. Yes, he has a lover in Dallas, but he didn't mention it before because, he told me, he didn't want to hurt my feelings. We had some very good fucking on that motel bed. In the morning we drove to Boulder Beach, then looked at the Hoover Dam. We stared, sticky and sleepy, at the ugly catfish in Lake Mead, and stood on the state-line, one foot in Nevada and one in Arizona. Then took our separate ways, he to Needles to call on a friend before continuing his journey to Texas, I to the Grand Canyon. I was, as he had once forecast, a road-sign at which he paused, not the man with whom he was going to travel.

The rest of the trip: the Grand Canyon, the Painted Desert, Bryce's Canyon, the long green valley that runs up the middle of Utah and is its only fertile feature, a tribute to the dedication and hard work of Mormons—then to San Francisco via Reno and the Donner Summit. Last days in Los Gatos, the farewell parties, the goodbyes, the train journey from Oakland across America—through the Rockies to Denver, over the great plains to Chicago, northern New York, and the magnificent forests of New England; then a few days with friends on Cape Cod, and the flight home from Boston. Phil, in floods of tears on Oakland Station. I watched him, aghast.

I don't want to write about this. Anyway, I couldn't describe the Grand Canyon; it's impossible, and there has been enough, or too much, scenery in this book already. But the Great Salt Lake reminded me of something I had written long ago, a poem that mourned the end of a difficult, disordered seven-year relationship, far from the pretty Temple and the gay Latter-Day Saints I had met:

> *It was an extraordinary phenomenon,*
> *Bizarre as comets with twelve tails*
> *Or small green men climbing from saucers—*
> *An obvious omen, but I*
> *Ignored the oracle, the thunder.*
>
> *Rain in the Salt Desert, on salt so hard and stacked*
> *And packed it could not drain away*
> *But lay, a new Arctic Sea, polar*
> *With icebergs and hot frost. Lightning*
> *Cracked; thunder thumped from clouds like bruises.*
>
> *Stetson, denim shorts, skin brown as mahogany,*
> *Money, a car and freedom, I,*
> *Outside and inside my eye, only*
> *Saw canyons, deserts, dead lake beds,*
> *Mist off the Sierra Nevada*
>
> *Lift at sunrise, raking summits and centuries*
> *Of snow. I wept, the Panamints,*
> *As hot and dry as Venus, were so*
> *Barren and beautiful. The salt*
> *Flats storm warned of an era ending:*

Five thousand miles away in a Torquay hotel,
At the same moment, you were in bed with
Another man. Well . . . nothing much of
Importance in that fact. Except
You fell in love with him; I lost you.

Sufficient to report that the Grand Canyon produced a sense of disbelief similar to the Las Vegas strip at night, curious though that may seem. I thought, once again, that my eyes had made a mistake. I walked away, then returned to look into that stupendous drop, and found, in an absence of only a few minutes, that my mind had already adjusted it, shrunk it into some measure of things to which I'm used. My mind was wrong. It was much vaster than my brain, retrospectively, said it was. Nor could I begin to put into words its extraordinary beauty, and the same is true of the colours of the Painted Desert, though perhaps if I lived near either for as long as I did in San Francisco, I would make the attempt. I gave a ride through the Painted Desert to a young Navajo Indian who was hitch-hiking some immense distance to see a girl. I still wear the necklace of beads he gave me. Dusk found us miles from anywhere, so I curled up with him in his sleeping-bag under the stars. I retain as one of my most vivid and meaningful pictures of America this man in the desert night, more at one with his surroundings than I could ever be, stroking my skin and talking about Navajo customs; while I, to satisfy his curiosity as we drank Olympia beer, smoked marijuana and made love, tried to explain Castro life and teaching at San José. All the paradoxes of California seemed to draw together in those moments. Meaningful, I said. It wasn't meaningful. It just . . . was.

It had no more meaning than the crunchy crystals and hideous dust of Death Valley, or any fragments I've noticed that appear to have urgency, that demand to be recorded—a woman in Glendale watering her garden with a hosepipe, a black preacher I met on a train who told me of her fears of flying, Avril as she walked down a corridor reminding me of Christmas trees. The stalagmites of Mono may suggest the salt pillar at Sodom, or Angelino smog warn of doom, the steel threads of the Golden Gate seem to stitch the two halves of California together; but they do none of these things: these are metaphors from my mind. The tufa, the petrol fumes, the bridge just simply are. So it is with the notes scraped on catgut that move me in a piece of music, the gesture of dancers at a disco, sex, the finite nature of all relationships. California has no meaning, however hard I try to find one, bring its extremes into some scale I can understand. It just is. It says, not try and understand me, but experience me, enjoy me.

I guess I did that.

Out of the Winter Gardens

David Rees

David Rees's latest novel describes the excitements and problems confronting a teenager as he moves from childhood to adolescence. As a 16-year-old, his first experiences with girls, his first trip abroad, and especially his discovery that his father is gay, force him to shake up his ideas about sexuality and the whole "grown-up" world. This book is a tender exploration of the father-son relationship.

David Rees's writing has been variously described as "crisp, economical . . . carries the narrative along" *(Times Literary Supplement)* and "once begun, difficult to put down" *(Time Out)*.

The author is a much-published writer of stories for and about young people, *The Milkman's On His Way* being the best-known. In 1978 he was awarded the Carnegie Medal (UK) for his novel *The Exeter Blitz*, and in 1980 he won the Other Award (UK) for his historical novel *The Green Bough of Liberty*.

Paperback, 128 pages, ISBN 0 946889 03 1, £3.50/$6.50.

Alphabet City

David Price

As his marriage disintegrates in a welter of suspicion and accusation, Peter begins to discover a homosexual identity of which he was previously unaware. He tries to escape his past and recreate his identity by fleeing to America. There he is drawn into the bleak sub-culture of Lower Manhattan and at the same time into a devouring relationship with Joe, a black actor. The two of them undertake a dangerous journey through the South-Western States, a journey of pursuit, self-discovery, and self-destruction . . . But Peter finds that his past is not so easily left behind.

"David Price has extracted the heart of New York and delivered it alive and throbbing on the page. This is the underworld that few tourists ever see . . . David Price has seen it with great clarity" (*Edmund White*).

"The novel's core, of a man launching out in search of transcendent passion, is winningly and sharply presented" (*Time Out*).

Paperback, 128 pages, ISBN 0 946889 00 7, £3.50/$6.50

The Scent of India

Pier Paolo Pasolini

"Moment by moment, there is a smell, a colour, a sense which is India". So wrote Pasolini in this collection of essays describing his visit to India with fellow authors Alberto Moravia and Elsa Morante. This book captures the shimmering, magical quality of India, while at the same time Pasolini's critical eye records the terrible poverty that accompanies it.

Though widely admired as a film director, Pasolini's talents as a poet, essayist and social critic are not generally known outside Italy. His ability to portray the dreamlike yet earthy quality of a country, which showed so clearly in his films, comes through in this book.

Paperback, 96 pages, ISBN 0 946889 02 3, £4.95/$7.95

The Other Italy

David Price/Gotthard Schuh

Here is the Italy which many travellers seek but few ever find, a series of portraits of traditional Italian rural life, drawn by someone with an intimate knowledge of it. David Price shows us an Italy which is steadily disappearing but which has, never-theless, proved to have an extraordinary tenacity in the face of modern social and economic developments.

The book ends with a look at the Ruins Management of Pompeii, which is seen as a symbol of this other Italy, challenged by natural and man-made disasters, and yet somehow still surviving.

The essays are complemented by Gotthard Schuh's photographs taken in the 1940s and 1950s. Text and photographs combine to express nostalgia for an Italy which has almost passed away.

"Lovely book . . . a strong undying charm like a scent from the past" (*Literary Review*).

Paperback, 80 pages ISBN 0 946889 01 5, £3.50/$6.50